MW00458677

Holy
CURIOSITY

Holy
CURIOSITY

Encountering Jesus'
Provocative Questions

WINN COLLIER

BakerBooks
a division of Baker Publishing Group
Grand Rapids, Michigan

© 2008 by Winn Collier

Published by Baker Books
a division of Baker Publishing Group
P.O. Box 6287, Grand Rapids, MI 49516-6287
www.bakerbooks.com

Printed in the United States of America

All rights reserved. No part of this publication may be reproduced, stored in a retrieval system, or transmitted in any form or by any means—for example, electronic, photocopy, recording—without the prior written permission of the publisher. The only exception is brief quotations in printed reviews.

Library of Congress Cataloging-in-Publication Data
Collier, Winn, 1971-
    Holy curiosity : encountering Jesus' provocative questions / Winn Collier.
      p. cm.
    ISBN 978-0-8010-6833-1 (pbk.)
    1. Christian life. I. Title.
  BV4501.3.C6458 2008
  248.4—dc22
                                            2008025601

Unless otherwise indicated, Scripture is taken from the HOLY BIBLE, NEW INTERNATIONAL VERSION®. NIV®. Copyright © 1973, 1978, 1984 by International Bible Society. Used by permission of Zondervan. All rights reserved.

Scripture marked Message is taken from *The Message* by Eugene H. Peterson, copyright © 1993, 1994, 1995, 2000, 2001, 2002. Used by permission of NavPress Publishing Group. All rights reserved.

Scripture marked TNIV is taken from the Holy Bible, Today's New International Version™ Copyright © 2001 by International Bible Society. All rights reserved.

In keeping with biblical principles of creation stewardship, Baker Publishing Group advocates the responsible use of our natural resources. As a member of the Green Press Initiative, our company uses recycled paper when possible. The text paper of this book is comprised of 30% post-consumer waste.

green press INITIATIVE

To Wyatt and Seth, my sons, my joy.
You prove the kindness of heaven.
I pray you always have the courage to ask true questions,
And I pray your heart is bold and patient to listen for
God's reply.

The problem with Christians is that they have the answer
. . . but haven't lived the question.

Ron Austin

Contents

1

When Jesus
Calls Us Out

It is a great loss if we greet every day with clenched hands stuffed with our own devices. We will never know what is out there waiting for us if we don't extend an empty hand to the world and wait for the wonder to happen.

Daniel Holman and Lonni Collins Pratt

He felt like a caged rat, buried alive in a tiny boxlike container, three thousand feet under the earth for fourteen brutal days. He was desperate but he wasn't alone. In early April 2006 three Australian miners, Brant Webb, Todd Russell, and Larry Knight, were working in a century-old gold mine when an earthquake hit, killing Knight and trapping the other two in a cramped steel safety cage over half a mile from fresh air, buried by tons of rubble and rock. For two agonizing weeks Webb and Russell endured the suffocating confines of their claustrophobic space. The situation was dire, and with their lower bodies pinned by debris, they considered amputating their legs with box cutters if surviving required it.

Panic set in, and they coped with their terrifying impasse with humor and music. Trying to find a song they both knew the lyrics for, they settled on Kenny Rogers's "The Gambler," spending harrowing hours reminding the crushing, pressing earth around them that indeed you "got to know when to hold 'em, know when to fold 'em." Confined and shut in, the darkness and the distance from other people worked against their humanity. "I just thought I was a caged rat," Webb said. Realizing the very real possibility that they would never see their families again, they wrote messages of love and affection on their skin, the only parchment they had. Miraculously, the messages were unnecessary. On April 25, after two unthinkable weeks buried alive, they saw the hands of rescuers reaching down, pulling them out of the small hellhole that had become their temporary home.

Being trapped in a small place is a horrible state for the body. It is an even more ghastly state for the soul. Yet most of us find ourselves there at some point, when our fears have run rampant or our disappointments have mounted.

We have felt deep rejection. We have seen the darkness of our heart. We have been abandoned or betrayed or simply ignored. We know what it is to be buried under layers of shame. We have been in hiding, maybe we *are* in hiding, far from sunshine and fresh air, like a caged rat. The paradox of our deep-earth dilemma is that, while we never would have chosen this solitary darkness, we *are* choosing it, day by suffocating day. We are too afraid of being hurt . . . *again*. We are too afraid of hoping . . . *again*, disappointed . . . *again*. And so we do what fearful people do. We hide. It might not look like hiding at all. We might talk a steady stream or wear an exquisitely crafted smile. We might take on some manageable role—the group jester, the profound thinker, the dutiful wife, the dependable husband, the melancholy cynic. But all these masks are only assorted ways of hiding. We might not see it but we are incredibly self-saturated, engrossed in the smallness of ourselves. And if we live here long enough, we grow quite used to being trapped in a small, small place.

I have a friend who has known true tragedy in his life. He has many reasons to grieve and good cause to be angry. However, he hasn't grieved well, and he doesn't allow his anger the space to boil so it can be tended to within the context of good friends and loving community. My friend has resorted to hiding and sulking and sabotaging relationships, places where he could be known in the very ways for which he longs. He is used to his smallness, content with his cramped space. I want to have the courage (and the permission) to ask him a straightforward question: Are you bored with yourself yet? It seems to me that a blunt question, aimed at the heart, from one who truly loves, would provide the best chance at jarring us from the hellholes into which we so readily descend.

I came to this conviction by way of personal experience. During graduate school, I ran headlong into my addictive perfectionist tendencies. I was hard on myself and hard on those I most deeply loved. One result of my neurosis was a near nervous breakdown. Many days I couldn't eat and merely endured the hours between opportunities to sleep. I was distant from my family, withdrawn, and dour. I was hiding and hiding quite well.

One night a mentor asked me a most unwelcome question. "Winn, are you willing to be wrong?" He touched a nerve. His meddling question dug down into my small space and curled up next to me. It would not be ignored; it forced me to ask how long I would exist closed off and self-consumed.

"So, Winn, are you bored with yourself yet?" There have been many occasions when such questions have arrested my attention. Another I remember well is when a friend asked me how I wanted my boys to remember me when I am gone. I can't think of any question that gets to my deepest longings and most crushing fears more than a question like that. It won't allow me the small space. It calls me out into the wild open. It calls me to live.

To live—truly live—requires courage. It is a dangerous thing to step into the untamed world where disappointments and tragedies and shame and sin run free. It takes a bit of moxie and more than a little nerve to shrug off the fear and the guilt and run with a devil-may-care abandon. If we give ourselves fully to hope, chances are that some mishap will crush our spirit. If we surrender to the chaos we have previously committed to hold at bay, good odds are that some terror will find its way to us. If we yield to desire, we run the risk of finding ourselves knee-deep in all sorts of scandalous behavior. So we often surmise it is more important to guard against these unfavorable outcomes than to dive into the unpredictable mess. However, we have named our breathing of this air and our movements on this sod an unambiguous word: *living*. And living is more than existing, more than hiding and hoarding, more than self-protection, more than guarding ourselves from the phobia of what might be. The word *living*, when spoken rightly, carries with it a hint of danger, a sense of awe. To live is a courageous act.

And it was precisely this—life—that Jesus said he brought to humanity. He stepped onto dusty soil, where little that he encountered could be called, in any true sense, life. Here he collided with a world long plunged into the fall, strangled by death, heaving and gasping in a spiraling darkness. Jesus' mission was to give himself over to the brutality of a Roman cross, and every redemptive act Jesus offered (and offers) finds its power in that cruel moment when God went silent and the sky turned black.

It is sometimes difficult, however, to find meaningful comfort in the abstract realities of Jesus' death-embracing and life-generating sacrifice. I need something more particular. I need a conversation. I need a touch. I need Jesus, God with flesh and bones. How did Jesus, God walking among us, speak against the death and the darkness and the loneliness and the shame? How did he seek to pull us into redemption as he met us on the street or shared a meal with us? How did he call us to emancipation when he faced our tears or our vice or our panic? Often Jesus used a simple, subversive power.

Jesus used a question.

Jesus' questions probed the soul, and they were not easily ignored. He posed one question to a grieving sister emptied of hope. He directed one toward a friend who couldn't muster up the courage to trust, and another toward the ears of a band of piously religious hypocrites. On another occasion, he questioned an invalid who seemed to prefer to wallow in regret rather than take the risk to believe.

These Jesus-questions refuse to stay put in dusty Palestine. They make an unsettling turn—toward us. Originally posed to distant people on a far-distant day, these questions, as all Jesus' questions do, get personal and begin to meddle. We find ourselves the characters in these stories—the grieving sister, the fearful friend, the power-crazed hypocrite, the wallowing invalid. Finding our place with them, we discover that Jesus' questions—first tossed in their direction—become our own disorienting, gracious queries. This soul work, this asking of true heart-deep questions, is an art we learn from Jesus.

Jesus is well aware we have our own questions, and he knows the raw and honest ones have always been a vital element of an authentic and alive spirituality. The wisdom writers knew it too. They lead us down the path of offering all we are to God, even those unsavory portions—our doubts, anger, complaints. Honesty is more important than pleasantry. If we are distrustful of God, it is ours to own. If we doubt God is real, we have to say as much to him. We can pull no punches. We cannot dance around the harder stuff, nor soften the vocabulary. If God's silence bewilders us, then *bewilder* must be the word God hears from us. If anger is what we feel toward God, anger must be what God feels from us. Far from the unleashing of emotional temper tantrums, this is merely a commitment to candor. If God is real, then God already knows the truth about us—all the truth—and it is the ultimate dishonoring of another to hide the sickness and ugliness erecting barriers to our giving and receiving love. When we pose our questions, particularly the darker ones, to God, it can be an act of faith, perhaps the greatest act of faith. Questions can be a way of tenaciously holding on to the core conviction that God is good and reliable and strong, big enough to handle even our mistrust. Jesus is comfortable with our questions, and he knows that our questions (at least the honest ones) are good and necessary.

But Jesus has a few questions of his own.

If our questions become the goal, we are no longer being honest but merely using our questions to hide. This will never do. Jesus will not leave us in our smallness. He does not want us to flounder in the suffocating space of humiliation or cynicism or dread. He will stand, firm and solid, and ask an unnerving question, inviting us to allow the question to have its impact, to unsettle us, to toy with our paradigms and shift the certain, steady ground we cling to so desperately. He will use the question to call us past our obsession with safety. Jesus' questions make us wiggle and squirm; they call us out.

When my son Wyatt was three, he had an interesting view of reality. He was learning how he was connected to his world, that he has a history and that he had not always been—and would not always be—three. Add a little imagination and a preschooler's philosophical wit to the mix, and you have something of a budding "circle of life" approach to metaphysics. Wyatt placed himself in most every event and imagined himself to have at one point been most every creature.

During the throes of summer, when mosquitoes were aplenty, Wyatt was the local mosquito population's favorite entrée. One day, while we were salving the multitude of bites on his legs, Wyatt said, "Daddy, when I was a mosquito, I would bite legs."

Wyatt's imaginative sense made for some interesting inquiries. One day he asked me where God was. "Everywhere,"

I answered, pleased I had offered a simple reply that still did justice to the ontological realities of the Almighty.

"But *where* is he? I can't see him," he insisted.

Where would I go from there, conversing with my three-year-old, when *everywhere* as an answer would not do? Wyatt's question pushed past the easy, the trite. His question forced me, sitting on my newly potty-trained son's bed, to acknowledge that his question was too big, and my words were too small: "Well, Wyatt, you're right. I can't see him all the time, either, and that is frustrating."

God's questions do the same, pushing us toward honesty and humility, refusing to let us hide behind stock answers.

After the tragedy of the fall, Adam and Eve hid. They hid their bodies and they hid their hearts. This is our introduction to sin. What began as Adam and Eve's stiff-necked rebellion quickly morphed into their rabid fear of being found out and a panic over their complete inability to decelerate the meltdown they had initiated. So Adam and Eve's response was to stick their fingers in their ears, close their eyes, and hum as loud as they could in the bushes, pretending they could hide from the truth. God stepped into the tragedy, though, and he posed a question: "Adam, where are you?" It was a question intended to unnerve them, to reveal their desperation, to call them out of their hiding.

God asked a question to the two hiding in the garden, and he has been asking questions to us ever since. His questions urge us out of our self-absorption and pull us into something far bigger: God. God's questions are subversive. They reframe the discussion. They are always at work pulling us out of ourselves and drawing us into himself. Ask Job or

Moses if God has ever used an intrusive question to serve his purposes.

Recently a friend who has journeyed with me through much of my own cynicism and wimpish behavior asked me if I was angry about it all yet, angry enough to move into action. He knew that as long as I huddled in the cramped but well-pampered and defensive space of distrust, fear had won. This defensive posture is too easy. Anyone can surrender his courage. Anyone can *not* believe. But to believe—to step forward even in our cowardice—to dare to risk and move, that is another thing altogether. That is the stuff hearty faith is made of, and Jesus will use powerful questions to spur us toward a hearty faith.

Jesus' encounter with the apostle Peter provides another example of this subversive nature of Jesus' questions. Peter was a volatile fellow. He lived in only two gears: all or nothing. He was either diving headlong into the storm-ravaged sea, full of confident faith, *or* he was sinking to the ocean floor, gasping with fear. He was either falling asleep, unable to stay awake at Jesus' request, *or* he was swinging his sword, single-handedly taking on the armed band arresting Jesus. Peter was wild. It is no surprise, then, that in Peter's most tragic hour, his sin was of the boldest sort: denying the Jesus he loved.

Common wisdom suggests that Peter's denial was fundamentally grounded in an effort to save his neck. Peter feared for his life, and so, in the middle of the high priest's courtyard

Holy Curiosity

where sentiment against Jesus had hit fever pitch, Peter denounced his friend. This might be so. But I read the story differently. Only hours earlier, Peter had risked his life for Jesus. When no one else moved to defend him, Peter pulled a sword. *Surely this is loyalty,* he must have thought. *Surely this is obedience to Jesus' description of noble friendship: one person laying down his life for another.* But Jesus' answer to Peter's bravery was rebuke. Peter had offered his life, and Jesus dismissed his act as misguided.

Adding to Peter's puzzlement, Jesus was now held captive by those intending to silence him once and for all. And Jesus did nothing. He wouldn't fight. He wouldn't let Peter fight. He just sat there, silent. *What sort of king is this?* Peter must have thought. Still, when nearly every other follower had deserted Jesus, Peter hadn't. He followed Jesus into the lair of the scheming religious leaders.

Peter was confused, no doubt. He was perplexed and anxious. However, with his ear-chopping fervor and his refusal to run, does it really seem plausible that Peter's strongest motivation was self-preservation? Or might it be that the one who had pulled the sword was driven by a dread of something other than death? Peter must have been engulfed in the bitterness of disappointment, doubts fueled by expectations ripped apart. Was Peter beginning to believe he had hoped in the wrong thing, the wrong one?

Warming by the enemy's fire, three critics posed Peter the most straightforward query: "Are you a follower of Jesus?" They did not ask what Peter thought of the Galilean's theology. They did not quiz him on the political positions of the carpenter turned prophet. They did not ask Peter if he believed Jesus' claim to be Messiah was a farce. Peter faced a more basic, less theoretical, inquiry. "Are you a follower?" Peter, doubting all he had experienced with Jesus, offered what might have been the most honest response available to him: "No."

Peter's betrayal was born of disillusion. The gloomy garden and the Judas kiss and Jesus' deafening silence in the face of it all were simply too much for Peter. And three times, all before the cock finished its crowing, Peter's confusion took shape in the form of a harsh, disillusioned *No*. He had no space for this sort of king, no category for this twist in the story. Peter's heart was good, but as with most of us, his "clenched hands [were] stuffed with his own devices." When what we expect will be is smothered by what actually *is*, doubts and clenched fists are our common response.

Peter's betrayal was odious. Though redemption came for Peter in the same way it is offered to us all, he will forever be remembered as the one who denied Jesus. This is a sad and unfortunate tale; yet if my read on Peter's place in the night before Good Friday is reasonable, I detect a sliver of respectability in Peter's disloyal hours: Peter *was* honest. Peter was angry. Perplexed and disappointed by Jesus' bizarre actions, Peter had more questions than faith. When asked if his loyalty lay with Jesus, he would not lie. Honesty of any sort, even the treasonous kind, is better than deception. The one barrier to redemption is refusing to own up to the darkness that led us to our humble place. Such refusal will keep us from falling before the feet of grace, which is precisely where Peter finds himself several days following his threefold denial.

When Jesus appeared to Peter after the resurrection, he didn't address Peter's treachery. Obviously Jesus had not been surprised by the denial; in fact, he had warned of its coming.

Jesus did not offer Peter a theological treatise on doubt and faith. He did not chide Peter for his seditious acts. Jesus chose a more subversive path. Rather than answer Peter's many questions, Jesus proffered his own: "Do you love me?" It's the sort of question that cuts to the center of things. It bypasses *should* and *why* and *how could you?* It digs deep for the rawest place. It is the sort of question that swallows you whole. With Jesus, the question takes shape; it becomes flesh and bones.

It is this flesh-and-bone rawness, this rich humanity of Jesus, that meddles with our callous, constricted hearts. Jesus does not ask a question—of Peter or of us—merely to make a point. The question is not just a rhetorical device, as if Jesus is merely pulling some tool out of his bag. Sometimes Jesus asks a question because he would really like to know the answer: *Do we love him?* It is a mystery how both true divine knowledge and true human inquiry mingle in one man, one God. But they do. The ancient catechisms insist as much. There is nothing more human, more honest, more inviting to friendship than a good soul-opening question. It cuts to the center, past the hubris. It carries love with it as it reaches into our depth. And the question lingers until we answer.

George Eliot surmises that animals make such good friends because they do not ask any questions and they do not offer any criticisms. If this criteria for friendship sticks, Jesus doesn't score well. The truth, however, is that a true friend is one who will sit with us in our emotional filth and our most disturbing neurotic fits, just sitting, perhaps with a faint hint of a smile. And then when the time is right, a true friend will offer a well-placed question, not one that manipulates or preaches, but one that invites us to peer deeper and to look harder, to wonder if repentance might be in order or hope might be embraced just past the chaos.

Jesus is such a friend, a strong friend with a fierce love. With the power and the hope and the sting of a well-placed question, Jesus calls us out of our smallness, out of ourselves. He calls us to open up our clenched fists, to embrace the wonder and to live—truly live.

My wife, Miska, is good at asking the well-placed question. Whenever I am in meltdown mode or living in obviously unhealthy ways, she likes to ask, "So, how's that working for you?" I hate that question. But it's a good one. It's the sort of question Jesus would ask.

2

Who Condemns You?

All the Mad Voices

> [O]f all the means to regeneration, remorse is surely the most wasteful. . . . It is a knife that probes far deeper than the evil.
>
> *E. M. Forster*

I'm not schizophrenic, but I've heard voices most of my life—shaming voices, judging voices, condemning voices. My guess is so have you.

Given my history, I find the story in John's Gospel of the woman caught in adultery engrossing. Yanking her from her lover's bed, the religious authorities dragged the woman to the temple courts where Jesus and all the people would see her humiliation. As this woman sat, like a lump in the dirt and in the middle of a gawking crowd, I imagine her own crushing guilt blended with the staccato slurs hurled from the frenzied mass. She must have been drowning, asphyxiated by the cacophony of accusation and denunciation. Sensing the overpowering chaos she was thrust into and connecting that to my own years of fending off condemning assaults, I am irritated by a question Jesus asked her, out loud and in front of the crowd: *Who condemns you?*

"Everyone!" I want to scream. "Don't you hear the accusations?"

Our world runs on condemnation. Parents discover their kids' behavior can often be modified with the threat (implicit or not) of Mom or Dad's emotional withdrawal and disapproval. Our culture's consumerist enterprise pushes its agenda on us with a steady stream of advertised condemnations, judging our large or skinny or flat or pimply body, judging our old car, judging our outdated clothes, judging our cheap vacation. It's sad that the church chimes in as well: "Do more. Be more. God sees you—aren't you ashamed of yourself?" One wonders if our whole world would gulp and misfire and grind to a knocking halt if it ever ran out of the fuel condemnation provides.

A few weeks ago Wyatt had his first day of kindergarten. As we prepared him for his new world, I had a man-to-man with him. I talked to him about holding on to who he is, protecting others in his class who might get picked on, and resisting that constant tug to always go along with the crowd (a bit over the top for kindergarten, but it was my first time too). We ended up role-playing a scenario where a few K-5 thugs were ganging up on a smaller kid. I told Wyatt that the bruisers were taunting the undersized boy and, to make the scene truly vicious, I added that the bullies called the boy "stupid." Wyatt made me proud, jumping up and mimicking how he would come to the distressed boy's aid. However, when we were done, Wyatt told me the whole event was entirely implausible. "No kids at school would ever call someone *stupid*," he said confidently.

Far too quickly, Wyatt will discover how wrong he is. Wyatt will hear many wounding words in this harsh world. The woman in John's tale certainly had. Condemnation was spewed on her from every conceivable angle. In addition to the condemnation prompted by her own poor choices, the shamed woman was also a victim of warped societal values, an unbending and coercive religious code, and the colluding schemes of a few power-crazed men. Left to herself, this woman didn't stand a chance.

John's narrative is unique because, while there is general agreement among biblical scholars that it is not part of the original text of the Gospel (and noted as such by brackets and a short explanation in most Bibles), there is also moderate consensus that this is a historical Jesus event. Could it be that it is one of the only noncanonical Jesus-stories preserved for the modern ear? Perhaps.

According to John, the Jewish religious leaders had grown irate with the carpenter from Galilee who was saying wild things and gathering a following. Jesus' message and way challenged their power structure, and they would have none of it. Determined to trap him, somehow, to get him to say or do something that would turn either the people or the Roman government against him, the religious leaders concocted a plan. They cornered a promiscuous woman, a woman who was either cheating on her husband or a harlot by trade. Bursting in on the affair, the plotters snatched up the woman and hauled her off to the temple courts to find Jesus, who was up at dawn, teaching. The boisterous mob poured into the courtyard, dragging the woman with them.

This was a sham. Certainly the woman had indulged in an illicit dalliance, but she had been set up. Whether the man she slept with was involved in the deception or whether the religious leaders had somehow gained information about the clandestine rendezvous, we do not know. However, the man's absence from the scene with Jesus is striking. Mosaic law, the ethical code that the Pharisees were supposedly honoring with this farce, required both partners in unlawful sex to be punished. Yet this mob had no concern for the man. They did not care about the law or justice. They cared only about turning the crowd against Jesus.

It is suspicious that this gang, religious leaders with families and lovers of their own, would have gathered together, early in the morning, to deal with a wayward woman. The religious leaders must have huddled near the secret meeting place, their greed every bit as lusty as the man who used the woman's body that night. Their informant gave them the word, and they barged into the house to find two naked bodies. Terror must have struck the woman. She had been found out. As they grabbed her by her hair and her arms and dragged her out of the house and into the street, barely clothed, what was happening inside her? As they pulled her past her neighbors' homes and through the market, how did she handle the stares? What did she do as the men snickered and as the mothers covered their young sons' eyes? What shape did her fear take when she saw the temple ahead, when she realized they were taking her there, to the holy place? As the men flung her down in the courtyard, she lay like a piece of trash crumpled in the dirt, her tangled hair covering her face.

With frantic energy, the men who had discarded the woman at Jesus' feet asked him what they should do with her. This was how they would ensnare Jesus. The crowd was drawn to his radical message of mercy and forgiveness, but the law was clear. The woman deserved death. If Jesus insisted on mercy, the religious adherents would turn on him, finally convinced he was in fact a heretic. If he called for death, the crowd would believe he had surrendered his role as the subversive prophet who offered grace to the afflicted. *What would Jesus do?*

What I find most disturbing is how such fierce and violent condemnation came at the hands of spiritual leaders. Contrary to popular caricatures, I don't believe the Pharisees (on the whole) were greedily consumed with power merely for the sake of power. I don't think they were wholesale charlatans, their external piety masking what was in truth a brazen disregard for Scripture and compassion. Somehow, though, these God-fearing men had become brutal oppressors.

The Pharisees lived in a nervous, tumultuous time. The Roman Empire challenged their national identity. The Sadducees, among others, were putting severe stress on Jewish theological boundaries. In response, the Pharisees desired to maintain their spiritual identity, an honorable enough cause. However, mixed with this noble pursuit, the Pharisees were increasingly motivated by fear. They wanted desperately to hold on to what they knew. They were comfortable when their traditions and structures were well marked and impregnable. They had created an image (and a theology) of God that would fit nicely with their desire for order. It is no surprise then that when Jesus came along, seemingly wild and unmanageable, he became yet another enemy who threatened their way of life.

The Pharisees had no real beef with the woman. In the wrong place at the wrong time, she was only the bait the religious leaders used to set a trap for Jesus. Is it shocking that these men of God would employ such evil means to do what they believed was God's work?

It shouldn't shock us. We do it. Why has the church poured such venom on the homosexual community? Is it really because of our deep concern for righteousness, or might it have something to do with the fact that we are terrified when we see same-sex couples walking down the streets holding hands? Are our "culture wars" truly emerging from a deep love to see truth and hope thrive in our world, or are these skirmishes more an opportunity for us to defend our established way of life against those we think would rip it from us? If love does motivate us, then why don't issues like our neighbor's poverty or loneliness or malnutrition (all biblical concerns) trigger in us the same emotional energy? Are we vexed only by those perils that threaten our comfort? Have we, like the Pharisees, used God's name (and disjointed fragments of God's truth) to crush and condemn people God loves, all so we can maintain a secure equilibrium? Jesus spoke harsh words against the religious elite who took meticulous care for the pedantic minutia of biblical code but had "neglected the more important matters of the law—justice, mercy and faithfulness." Jesus called them hypocrites. Would he say the same of us?

I know I've handed out this kind of condemnation. On a few occasions, I've received it. I was in junior high when I attended a youth camp that was obsessed with sex. I remember one particular evening devoted to the topic. Guys sat on one side; girls on the other. There were slides and scary statistics. One of the main features was a fire-and-brimstone presentation on the subtle pervasiveness of male gay culture. I was fairly naive and probably did not fully understand what a gay guy was (and certainly had no clue what a gay guy *did*). No matter. To hear the leaders rant, they must have thought I was on the verge of joining up. They offered many irrefutable indicators of how virtually every one of us guys was dabbling in perversion: hairspray, layered shirts, pink shirts, of course. And, most damning—parting our hair down the middle.

I remember all this because I parted my hair down the middle—and one of my favorite shirts for the week was my crisp, pink oxford. One evening I was combing my hair in the guy's bathroom, as a youth pastor washed his hands in the sink next to me. He stared at my hair and my shirt, and then with a grave tone, he asked if I knew the kind of evil I was participating in. It angers me to remember the rebuke and the condemnation I felt. How dare that authority figure unload on my adolescent psyche his fear of a world run out of his control?

Ruthless as the words and dishonest schemes of the spiritual leaders were, the woman thrown at Jesus' feet needed little prodding to feel condemned. As anyone who bears condemnation will tell you, self can be the worst abuser. My guess is that the condemnation the religious lynch mob flung

Holy Curiosity

at her landed on a tall pile she had been building for years. Self-condemnation (shame) usually starts externally: a mom who can never simply say (and mean), "You are good," or a spiritual leader who can never simply say (and mean), "You've done enough." Though the impetus begins on the exterior, the negative perception of ourselves that these encounters produce settles in and becomes a piece of us. I don't need someone to tell me I'm evil or that my dark places make me disgusting. I say it to myself quite well, thank you very much. And often.

After the woman had been dropped in the dirt in the middle of the temple square, she sat stone still and quiet. She didn't dare look, but she heard the name *Jesus* whispered. She knew he was a prophet, and she was humiliated to be here with him. This degradation was more than a human soul could bear. She was sinful and she was ashamed. Yet her shame must have come from more than her sin.

Was she ashamed of her womanhood? To these powerful men, she was *only* a woman, expendable for the greater cause. In a culture where women were told never to forget their place—in a culture where a woman could be in this predicament while the offending man was nowhere to be found—it must have been almost impossible to hold on to her dignity and worth.

I wonder if even her sexual choices hint at the shame she had long imbibed. In a civilization where a woman's only real asset was her virginity and her sexual fidelity, why had she surrendered so much for so little in return? Why had she abandoned her dignity so readily? What lies and abuses had led her here? As she groveled in the dirt, her soul must have shriveled and retreated.

Shame has a way of shutting us down.

One Saturday night, Miska and I had a horrific conversation. We were in bed, and it was just about time to click off the lights and call it a day. Earlier she had seemed lethargic and unresponsive to me, and so I asked her what was happening inside her. Her answer caught me off guard, as when a doctor distracts with his left hand and plunges a needle with the right. "I don't know you anymore," she said. "The spark is gone. It's like there is a ghost of you walking around."

Shame had pushed me to this phantom place. My condemning voices had been chattering incessantly, slinging rapid-fire accusations: *You are worthless. You are vile. If others knew what was happening in your head right now. . . . You will never be free of this.* The longer I listened, the more of a ghost I became. I wanted only to hide. But hiding will never work.

Before his 1970 divorce from Canadian actress Shirley Douglas, Donald Sutherland hit a rough stretch and was broke. He had only one pair of black pants, and they had a nice rip right in the seat. Sutherland didn't want to ask for his wife's help to sew them up. So, according to his son Kiefer, he just painted his derriere black to match. I doubt the paint covered him up as well as he hoped.

Try as we might, some of our soul's bare spots are impossible to truly cover. Left unresolved, our self-condemnation will only grow louder, shouting at us and intimidating us until we shrivel up and shut down.

Holy Curiosity

These shrill, incessant voices heaping heavy loads of condemnation on us are liars. God never piles on shame. God never assaults our personhood. He never speaks with hopelessness or despair. God *will* correct and instruct. God will tell us the truth, even if it hurts. God always works to get our attention and remind us of our true, powerful, beautiful name. But God never—ever—heaps condemnation on us. *That* is the devil's work.

Still, we cannot ignore the fact that this woman was in this predicament, in part, because of her own sinful choices. This is how condemnation gains a foothold with us: it speaks a half-truth. Condemnation *does* give credence to our miserable condition, reminding us we are sinful and broken. However, even though condemnation at times may rightly point at our sin, it never offers a way out. Condemnation turns us inward, toward self-flagellation. We begin to loathe who we are, using self-hatred in a vain attempt to offer penance for our many failures. The entire downward spiral is a failed enterprise, however, because, as Frederick Buechner says, "It is about as hard to absolve yourself of guilt as it is to sit on your own lap."

From its very beginning, condemnation has nothing to do with Jesus, nothing to do with the gospel. The scandal of grace is that God came to us because we are bad, evil, desperate. God did not pursue us because our perfections were so attractive but because our malady ran so deep. Condemnation ignores this truth, runs right past it. Self-obsession acts as though the gospel is unnecessary. Jesus came to us, for us, in our "helpless estate," in no way surprised by the mess he found us in. This is the gospel story, but condemnation knows nothing of it.

Some of us can't shake condemnation because it is the inevitable corollary of believing the illusion of our own inherent goodness. Condemnation, for all its faults, does reinforce ideas we find most addictive: that we should be able to make ourselves good and that we have at least the capacity to right our own ship. To be rid of condemnation, we must believe the brutal truth. We are in miserable shape, and Jesus is our one and only hope. But those are hard truths to own. This must be the reason Bonhoeffer believed that, of all the world's idols, guilt was the hardest to topple.

So what would Jesus do? How would he answer the question the men asked about how to handle the adulterous woman? The silence was tense, as all those who had gathered waited to hear the Prophet's reply. Here the narrative begins to offer intriguing details on Jesus' precise bodily movement. Rather than answering the crowd's question, oddly, the text tells us Jesus bent down. He felt no compulsion to respond. He just bent down and allowed the tension to settle in. His deliberate movement, along with his refusal to give the answer everyone waited for, provided a reminder that Jesus was in charge. The many onlookers must have shuffled a bit, looking around for someone, anyone, to know how to get this Jesus to answer the question.

After the awkward moment, Jesus began to write in the dirt. Actually, the verb describing this writing action in the text is a bit ambiguous. It could mean *to write*, as in the writing of words or characters, or it could mean *to draw*, as in pictures or symbols or markings of any sort. Speculation about exactly what Jesus was doing is endless. Was he purposefully giving himself time to ponder? There was a Semitic custom of doodling when one was confronted with heavy thoughts.

Was he practicing the tradition of Roman judges who would write down a decision before announcing it? Was he writing some Scripture passage? Some have suggested he might have written down a line from Exodus 23:7: "Have nothing to do with a false charge," an immediate warning to the religious crowd. Perhaps the most enduring speculation is that Jesus wrote the sins of the woman's accusers in the dust for all to see, much to the horror of the religious leaders who were being publicly exposed. Perhaps he scribbled the names of her other lovers, some of the same men who had dragged her there. Whatever Jesus wrote, this is sure: he took command of the moment, making the accusers wait and allowing their lust and their schemes to ripen. He was demonstrating his quiet, unhurried, firm authority over the situation, just bending down and drawing in the dirt, as everyone waited to see how it would play out.

Then Jesus moved a third time. John made certain to tell us that Jesus stood up. Jesus rose to break his silence and speak firmly, directly to the horde of men. "If you have no sin, then you be the first to hurl a stone." What could they do with that? Jesus spoke all he cared to speak—that was enough; and he knelt back down. The accusers must have twitched and brooded, trying to figure out how to respond. Then nothing. One by one, they walked away.

The courtyard was quiet now. It must have been strange, only Jesus and the woman. "Where are they?" Jesus asked. "Who is left here that condemns you?"

"No one," she answered. No crazed men, no ogling crowd, no raised stones, no shame, no reason to hide—it was quiet, beautifully quiet, and she was alone.

Yet she was not alone. The woman's sin was no less apparent, her past no more innocent, her brokenness no less obvious. But here Jesus stood, and—this must not be missed—he had remained there all along. The woman might not have sensed it, amid all the insults and the fury; but while the crowd kept their distance, only close enough to leer and taunt, Jesus held his space, next to her. She had a friend in the middle of her shame, and still this strong Friend stood there. This strong Friend wanted to know—he wanted to hear from her own lips—if there were any condemners left.

No. No one.

I wonder if she still feared what Jesus might do. She was of course fully aware of her own sinful choices. And here she was, half-clothed in the middle of the street, her sin obvious to the world . . . and God stood only a few feet away. This is the real question: What would the One who actually had the right to accuse her say now?

"I do not condemn you either," said Jesus. What else is there to say—who else has anything to say—when Jesus does not condemn us? "Go and stop sinning; go and live free," he told her. And this is what he tells us. Be free! Free from the voices of our past, free from the condemning words we speak to ourselves, free to live.

The condemning voices are legion, but when Jesus speaks—if we will hear him—the voices are all silenced. Every single one! "It is the Sovereign Lord who helps me. Who is he that will condemn me?"

Why Are You Afraid?
The Grace of Letting Go

I abandon You, Lord.
I question Your goodness,
by yielding to evil cravings
and weakening myself with harmful fears.

Thomas Aquinas

People fear miracles because they fear being changed.

Leif Enger

In the Deep South where I live, we have an annual summer pariah. Kudzu looks something like ivy but spreads so fast, you measure its progress by the hour. I've seen kudzu take over twenty-foot utility light poles, carpet an entire hillside, and, most astonishingly, devour an abandoned car parked too close to the woods. Kudzu works steadily, consistently. You really don't notice what is happening, a sprout here and an intruding vine there; but all of a sudden, you look out at your front yard and it's gone, gobbled up—kudzu everywhere.

Fear is the heart's kudzu. It works fast, and it aims to consume us. Fear, says writer Yann Martel, "has no decency, respects no law or convention, shows no mercy."

Matthew tells a story of a murky, tempestuous night when fear consumed Jesus' disciples. The disciples and Jesus were on a fishing boat late in the evening; Jesus was asleep. Without warning, a fierce storm hit the Sea of Galilee. Matthew called it a "furious storm," a *seismos* as the Greeks put it. Usually *seismos* referred to an earthquake and often implied an apocalyptic cataclysm. This was not just wind and bluster. A vicious torrent descended on this small band of men trapped in the middle of the angry sea. And they were terrified.

Several of these men were fishermen. They had seen their share of storms and had been through more than a few strong gales. I don't know when last you spent time in a fishing village, but the men and the women who run those boats are anything but timid. They're salty folk. This storm, however, was a different beast, and the disciples weren't going to be able to ride it out as they always had before.

Life has a way of pushing right past the boundaries we construct. Tragedy and heartache don't play by the rules. We might maneuver long enough so that we begin to believe we possess the courage to navigate whatever we will meet, but then a *seismos* comes—a late night call from the police, a bankruptcy, a child with an incurable disease, an AIDS crisis, famine, poverty. And we are terrified.

Terrified, the disciples rushed to Jesus, stunned to find him asleep in the middle of the mayhem. Awaking to the brutal storm and the terror-stricken faces, Jesus asked a question that seems absurd. *Why are you afraid?* Well . . . there was the crashing wind whipping the boat like a toothpick in a hurricane. There were the monsoon-like waves roaring so loudly the men could barely hear themselves scream. There was the fact that every instinct told them they would never see land again. Yet Jesus asked them why, exactly, it was they were afraid.

It is important for us, when grasped tightly by fear, to slow our breath and ask ourselves this same question—what *exactly* is it we are afraid of? When we are able, we should work to name our fear, to trace the sensation back to its home. A churning stomach or a mind run offtrack or hair raised on our neck should prompt us to ask: Why?

Fear has many common instigators: hairy spiders, disorienting heights, public speaking, enclosed spaces. Fear also comes from the rawest wounds of our soul: the father who never showed us how valuable we were, the years of being the outsider at school, the boss who said we were useless, the sin that left long scars. From these places and because of these voices, we live afraid, running away and trying to prove or protect ourselves.

Often fear manifests itself in inconspicuous ways we would not immediately recognize—but fear lurks even there. Isn't the humorous cynic fearful of hope? Isn't the adrenaline junkie who will try anything, do anything, often fearful of quiet and stillness? Looking back, I see fear in places I would not have admitted at the time. Why was I the high school class clown?

While some of us are aware of fear only in the rare experiences when we are under extreme duress, for others, fear is a second self. Some of us live with dread, just waiting for tragedy to occur. Our mind will not stop churning out the disastrous possibilities, and we grow cautious, unable to live and love freely. Some of us cannot—ever—shake the sense that we are going to make a fool of ourselves or that some evil will consume us, and so we silence our voice and crawl into a quiet, cautious space.

Fear, in its proper place, is a gift. It can keep us from making stupid choices, and it alerts us to the possibility of legitimate dangers. But too often fear gobbles up far more territory than it should rightfully possess.

When I was younger and my choices less significant, fear was a less noticeable problem. But as I grew older and my decisions and the consequences of those decisions grew larger—choosing a career and deciding to have kids—fear found a lot more raw material to work with. With each new decision, the stakes are raised. As essayist Timothy Stanley says, "Fear is part of us. It is the basic experience of facing unknown limits." But we shudder at the unknown and we strive to find comfort by managing our life, minimizing risk, and keeping a steady equilibrium. We want our marriage to work and our kids to stay healthy and our hopes to never be dashed too harshly. So we figure out what works and do it, an infinite quest to maintain a steady hand at the wheel.

Of the many words I could use to describe Branson, Missouri, *dangerous* is not one of them. Tucked away in a quiet corner of the Ozarks, Branson was once a small mountain town that has become a Mecca-like destination for people (mostly older) who love hillbilly music and outlet malls and pecan pralines and who possess abiding affection for Dolly Parton. Still, reputation aside, I was once terrified in Branson.

When I was in college, our family headed to Branson one summer for vacation. My sister Vonda, four years younger than me, has a bit of a wild streak, and as soon as we rolled into town, she spotted the Skycoaster, a bare steel tower looming one hundred feet off the ground. The Skycoaster is built for people with borderline personality disorders who find perverse pleasure in having their stomach slammed into their throat as they free-fall like a brick screeching toward the pavement. Of course, as soon as Vonda spotted the Skycoaster, she wanted in on the action. And she wanted me to join her.

Have I mentioned that I'm afraid of heights? I was the kid who stood frozen atop the pool's high-dive board, the kid whose mom (who, incidentally, can't even swim) had to climb up to initiate a rescue—only, my mom's "rescue" was to give me a shove off the board, but that's another story. I'm the guy who can't look down at the narrow slits between the boards of a suspended walkway. Nonetheless, because no self-respecting college guy can tell his little sister, *No, I will not ride the Skycoaster because I'm scared and might wet my pants*, I found myself in line holding a ticket and standing next to one very psyched-up sibling.

The Skycoaster attendants shoved us both into an enormous harness (imagine what a diaper for an elephant would look like) and then hooked us to a taut steel wire stretched to the top of the tower. One of the guys placed my hand on a red plastic handle and told me that when we reached the top, to count to three . . . and pull. Gravity would take care of the rest.

Pull? That's it?

We reached the top far too quickly. By that point, there were few options. We could stay there, staring at the asphalt far below, suspended in midair inside a large body diaper—or I could pull. But as soon as I pulled that cord, everything was out of my hands. Everything. The red handle offered only a small illusion of my ability to maintain control over my situation, but that illusion was all I had. I clutched that handle as though it were life itself, until eventually I had to pull the cord.

It seems to me the fear of being caught when I don't have a firm grasp on the situation prompts almost all my fears. This was certainly true on two other occasions when fear dug its claws into me. When I asked Miska to marry me, she responded by asking me (unfortunately, repeatedly) if I was *sure* about my decision. *Sure*—that's a tricky word for me, and immediately vicious fears of the unknown dug in. Another time, I was at the Dallas airport and had just boarded a plane headed for Venezuela. I had a summer break from graduate school, and I was embarking on a short-term mission trip. Just as I sat down, internal anarchy let loose. A frightful suggestion blindsided me. It was a question I couldn't answer, a vicious attack on my character, vile accusations about my identity and my desires. Immediately I felt out of control; and as a result, panic sent me spiraling.

Recently I watched a documentary called *The Darfur Diaries*. It chronicles the tragedy and genocide in Darfur, a western region of Sudan. The violence is sickening—genocide and bombs and rape and hunger and thousands of children who have lived horrors no human should ever know. Isn't there a part of us that would just rather not see these images or hear these stories? These faces and these cruelties are something we cannot manage.

The unnerving truth is that it isn't just the chaos in other places that we cannot manage. We are often helpless against the chaos present in the middle of our own immediate world. Fear is what happens when we finally come face-to-face with the brutality of life, and when we recognize that we are far too small to stop it from doing as it pleases. When this happens, we can lean into the fear, curious as to what we might uncover about ourselves, or we can exert vast amounts of energy trying to beat back the internal bedlam.

Most reads on this storm narrative hear Jesus' question of why the disciples were afraid as an unqualified reprimand. There must be something to this, particularly since Jesus pointedly asked them where their faith had gone. However, Scripture says that Jesus' rebuke was first leveled at the raging wind and waves, not the disciples. I don't hear Jesus' words to the Twelve as an irritated scold. It seems that Jesus calls his disciples out, calling them to see their fears for what they are, calling them to courage.

A fear that is ignored and constantly shoved to the edges is not defeated; it is merely given time to sharpen its fangs. Such fears must be invited to the light, and in this case, an invasive question was Jesus' invitation. His question was not an exasperated reaction to his disciples' fear. The truth is that God's sovereign control was not at all obvious. My hunch is that anyone who would chastise the disciples for having fear in this moment has simply not lived honestly enough, has simply not allowed the devastation of this world to come in close.

There is little mystery to the fact that the disciples were fearful in the middle of dark, raging, frothing waters that were ready to take them under. I understand why they were afraid. I am far more curious about why Jesus *wasn't*. One could quickly dismiss the whole query by asserting that Jesus is God and God doesn't get scared. Maybe. But was there no fear in Gethsemane when Jesus sweated blood and asked God to save him from the darkness to come? Was there no fear on the cross when Jesus cried out to the Father who had abandoned him? How can Jesus be one who has "been through weakness and testing, experienced it all" if he has not felt the sadistic power of fear? Is it possible that Jesus' correction of the disciples was not so much for *feeling* fear as it was for obeying it?

By the way Matthew pieced together this portion of the story, he was telling us something particular about Jesus. Matthew says that Jesus is one with authority. This observation requires no exegetical genius. Matthew said it plainly, that the "crowds were amazed at his teaching, because he taught as one who had authority." Matthew followed with several stories. The first was of a leper who approached Jesus, saying that if Jesus simply desired to heal him, he knew he would be healed. The leper appealed to the good heart of Jesus, knowing all that was needed was for Jesus to *want* to act. The authority to make it happen was of no concern.

The next story was of a Roman centurion who approached Jesus requesting him to heal his paralyzed servant. Jesus told the centurion that he would come to his house and perform the healing. However, the Roman official made bold statements about Jesus' authority, declaring that he knew the only thing needed was for Jesus to *say* it would be done—and it would happen. Next, as if to highlight how Jesus' influence was not limited to a few isolated individuals, Matthew listed entire groups of people, many who were demon possessed and multitudes who were sick, that Jesus healed. Jesus' authority was broad, limitless. It touched all who cared to be touched.

This theme weaves its way to the story of the storm-beaten boat. After Jesus woke to the barbarous conditions and his unnerved disciples, he stepped to the ship's edge and spoke words to the wind. He simply told the wind to stop. And it did. The disciples didn't know what to do with what they had just seen. "What kind of man is this?" they asked. "Even the winds and the waves obey him!"

Authority—it calms a storm and it is the only remedy for a fearful soul. Techniques are not what we really need. A pep talk to muster our resolve is not the answer. That is the stuff of self-help, continuing the delusion that our only requisite is just a more courageous version of ourselves. However, our real need is One far larger than us, One who will show us that we are not alone and that our fears are not the most powerful truth. We need a God large enough and strong enough to be in control of our precarious life.

In *Finding Neverland*, the wonderful cinematic portrayal of the friendship J. M. Barrie (*Peter Pan*'s creator) fostered with four fatherless boys, a poignant scene develops near the end. One of the younger boys, Peter (yes, there is a connection), had taken his father's death and his mother's subsequent terminal illness the hardest. At his mother's funeral, he ran away into the park so he could hide his emotions and attempt to cope. He resisted any person's claim on his trust, believing that his safety rested fully on his own shoulders. For Peter, his mother's death confirmed his darkest dread: he was in charge of his well-being.

As Barrie approached Peter sitting alone on a remote park bench, Peter struggled to push his short legs to the ground so he could launch from the bench and run farther away. But Barrie's voice, firm and direct, halted his efforts. "Peter, sit down," he said. The words were short and straightforward. Yet there was something in Barrie's eyes, something in his heart, something in the way he was stepping into Peter's chaos that was life-giving. Barrie's stance told Peter he was not alone. He was not in charge of his own safety. Barrie was stronger than Peter, and Barrie was there to help. But first, Peter would need to sit down.

This is a simple scene, a man telling a boy to take his seat on a bench. But it is much more. The boy was lost, alone. He needed someone bigger, someone with enough courage to step into his chaos. He needed someone strong enough to handle him and wise enough to know how and when to use his strength. So many times, I have been on that bench, a little boy wondering if there is anyone bigger than me, big enough to tell me I am not on my own. We have all sat there, and our heart yearns for another who is stronger and wiser to speak with authority, to speak words of hope and life.

Jesus' way of dispensing hope and life is strange. Rather than giving his followers reasons *not* to be afraid, Jesus multiplied their cause for fear. Immediately preceding the storm narrative, Jesus had warned that whoever followed him would not be assured of a place to sleep or be able even to attend to the established customs of caring for the dead. Foxes at least had a hole in the ground in which to burrow. Birds at least had a nest of scratchy twigs and dried-up leaves as shelter from the wind. Most every daughter or son had the capacity to bury his or her parents. These are scrimpy pleasures—sleeping and caring for the dead. Yet Jesus said that no one who followed him could depend even on these.

Jesus did little to provide calm. Rather, he tugged at his followers' fears, prodded, and provoked them. Following Jesus meant surrendering any assured solace in the most basic human acts. What sort of creatures are we if we are not granted good sleep and a good death? What is Jesus doing, pushing us to this place, pushing against boundaries, and eliciting fears? Isn't Jesus supposed to calm us? Isn't he supposed to tell us that everything will be okay? Perhaps God wants to move us to a deeper peace than we know, a deeper joy and rest than we have experienced—but perhaps we have to move through our insatiable fears of losing control to get there.

Jesus warned his followers that they might never have a place to sleep. Yet a few lines later, Jesus was in deep slumber amid cyclonelike conditions, as everyone else clutched anything solid to hold on to and frightfully muttered what they assumed were final prayers. This is a strange paradox. With Jesus you can never be assured of a safe place to rest your head, and yet with Jesus any place you can rest your head (even a wild, death-summoning storm) will do. Perhaps this is why we fear trusting God, because God, wild and unfettered, is completely out of our control.

So long as we hold on to our demands of what our life must look like, fear has an easy place to set its hooks. If we believe we must have tranquil waters and if we are committed to the concept of comfort, then fear finds fertile ground. Often fear is a result of our anxiety that some expectation, some ideal, some demand will not be realized. We fear someone or something will hurt us. We fear that we will be alone or insignificant or rejected. And here is the truth: we might. No. Someday, from some angle, we will. Have your moment. Face your fear. We must give ourselves to the truth that even sleeping and dying are out of our control.

I have recently wrestled through my rampant and irrational fears, and they have devoured far too much of my life. *How did I get here?* I ask myself. *I don't recognize me—this isn't who I am.* During one conversation, as I attempted to explain the insanity in my head, Miska replied simply, "Winn, this will never go away until you stop being afraid of it." It's a strange thing to say, isn't it—your fear will not diminish unless you stop being afraid? The truth is there, though. This is no mental sleight of hand, ignoring the truth of how I feel or insisting, as a matter of my will, that I'm not afraid when in fact I am. To say I must stop being afraid of something is not the same as saying I must stop feeling fear. Rather, it is an assertion that I will not surrender myself to it. I will not lie at its feet and grovel. Fear is not God, and I will not worship it. Fear might well be present, but I will not yield my obedience to it. I will stand square. I will look it in the eye. And even as terror grips my every fiber, I will not surrender my space. The presence and the way of Jesus call me to a different way, a firmer, more solid way.

Recently, during Lent, I felt God's nudge that it was time to do serious battle with my fear. It was time to stand up. It was time to assert the truths I claim—that the living Christ within me is more powerful than any fear or upheaval that has taken residence in my soul. Praying the Hours, the long church practice of praying daily fixed prayers at fixed times (or offices), would be part of my discipline to turn my heart toward redemption and hope. And so, on the first morning of my exercise, I opened to the morning office. And this call to worship greeted me: "Be strong and let your heart take courage, all you who wait for the LORD." Be strong. Be courageous. Jesus, our mighty, resurrected God, is coming. And, because my Redeemer is alive and powerful and moving on my behalf, I can stand firm and bold, alive and free.

This gritty posture is not something we muster on our own. Our courage grows firm as we submit to the authority and reality of Jesus. Our heart knows the truth: this world is a mess, and our life is always just on the edge of careening out of control. We are sinful. We will be disappointed. We can't deflect every evil and violence and tragedy. Ultimately, we cannot manage our life. We cannot manage our fears. Somewhere, somehow, they will push their way to the surface. We don't need another tip to help us maneuver our fears or another strategy to allow us to submerge them. Our desperate need is for another who is stronger than fear, more alive than fear. We need Jesus.

Make no mistake, the disciples were in trouble. They had every reason to fear. But the disciples had missed that Immanuel—God—was sleeping in the hull. God was with them, and God was at rest. The same is true for us. It would be a lie to say that there is nothing to fear. The truth, however, is that Jesus has stepped between us and our fears. He takes their fury.

We must ask ourselves if we believe God is with us in Jesus. We must ask ourselves if we believe Jesus truly has the authority to meet our fears head-on—and to speak against them, each and every one. It is true, as Aquinas taught us, that when God is with us, there is much that simply "ought not to be feared."

When Wyatt calls me upstairs to his room at night and tells me he is afraid, it does little good to tell him bluntly that there is nothing to be afraid of. It's true—there are no hairy, green monsters in the darkened corner, no malevolent shadows waiting to pounce. However, his fears come from deeper places. Wyatt fears he will be alone. Wyatt fears he will be left to himself to fend off the menace his imagination conjures up for him. Wyatt needs to know his dad and his mom are nearby. Wyatt wants to know that, as he says it, "If I *really* need something, you'll come up." So, even as I tell Wyatt that there are no monsters, I want to be quicker to tell him what he most needs to hear—that his safety is not in his own hands, that if any scary creatures are foolish enough to enter my son's room, his dad will be there, hell-on-wheels, faster than he can blink, to dish out a grade-A monster butt whoopin'.

So, in this instance, what Wyatt really needs are not tools to rationalize his fears away but rather to come face-to-face with his father's strength. And *this* is a conversation every dad was made for.

"Wyatt," I say, "you bet, buddy. If you need me, I'll be up here faster than lightning" (and in Wyatt's world, *nothing* is faster than lightning).

As Wyatt shows the first hints of a grin, I continue. "And you know what else? When I get up here, I'll crush every monster there is."

Wyatt is beaming now, quite excited actually. He likes the sound of this *crushing* stuff. "Do you know why you don't need to be afraid?" I ask.

"No," he answers, sitting up on his knees in his bed, wide-eyed and now half hoping a monster or two *would* saunter in.

"Because," I say, "your daddy is stronger than any monster there is."

Then I put Wyatt back under his covers where he can drift to sleep, dreaming about all the cool stuff his dad could do if he ever snagged one of those monsters in a headlock. Wyatt's fears are best tamed, not by an argument or a psychological technique, but by his dad's hand, his dad's voice, his dad's authority. Simply dousing fears really isn't the solution. Being present—that is the stuff of hope.

Holy Curiosity

"Incarnation is the place," says Kathleen Norris, "where hope contends with fear." Perhaps this hints at the reason, if Jesus was familiar with fear, he was not distraught in the boat that was battered by the ferocious storm. He was not afraid because he was aware of God the Father with him. Perhaps this also tells us why the cross evoked such a different, disquieted response from Jesus. There, as the sky turned black and as Jesus cried out as only a forsaken man could, God was nowhere to be found. That is a place of terror.

Christ has known ultimate fear. He has known fear in ways we never will. It is not that Jesus is unable to understand the range of our fears; it is that we are unable to understand the depth of his. We must resist any easy notion that Jesus never knew fear. This does injustice to his humanity, and it offers little hope when fear engulfs us. How can we say God is truly "with us" if he has not been at times immersed, like us, in the torrent of fear?

This God-incarnated, this blood-and-bone God-in-Jesus, came to "contend with fear." He did not come only to face nobly fear's blunt force . . . and die. Jesus' face-off with fear did not conclude on a darkened Friday when hope was lost and hell quivered with pleasure. After cross came resurrection, and in the mysterious hours between the two, Jesus took death and sin—all that makes up the foul side of fear—and placed them squarely under his crushing heel. Fear unleashed all it possessed on Jesus, a torrent of death and shame and abandonment and sin, enough to finish even the strongest of men. But fear did not destroy Jesus; Jesus destroyed fear.

Our comfort and courage do not come from a Jesus who was unmolested by fear; our comfort comes from a Jesus who went into fear's very bowels . . . *for us*. He drank in every acidic ounce of fright and distress and vexation. For us, he drank it in. And now, as he stands leaning toward us, Immanuel asks, "Why are you afraid?"

4

How Much Bread Do You Have?

Makings of a God Feast

There's a capacity for appetite . . . that a whole heaven and earth of cake can't satisfy.

John Steinbeck

You have therefore given me in my weakness Your sacred Body to be the refreshment of my soul and body. . . . Your Sacrament is the bread of my life.

Thomas à Kempis

We have lost much of our memory of the good Garden where lush fruit grew aplenty and where warm sunshine greeted us each day. There friendship with our God as well as our human lover was uninhibited, trusting; our heart was left ajar for love to flow freely back and forth. But we have forgotten. Now some of us seldom know what it is to be satisfied and content, to awake to dazzling joy, to be at peace with God and ourselves.

We haven't forgotten everything, mind you. How could we with this constant gnawing in the pit of our belly? Our hunger is ever with us, and though we try like mad, we cannot assuage it. We are trapped between two truths. Our soul was made for a feast, but most of our days offer famine.

Human hunger prompted one of Jesus' plainest questions. Matthew recounted the story of a large crowd (probably eight to ten thousand) that had followed Jesus into a remote wilderness. They had listened to his teaching for three full days, longer than anyone had expected. Unprepared, the crowd had already depleted the food they had with them. Jesus was concerned and knew the people needed to eat. Calling his disciples together, he presented the conspicuous dilemma, concluding with his expectation that the crowd be fed. When Jesus finished talking, he waited for a response. What were the disciples supposed to do with that?

If the biblical narrative were a screenplay, this is how I imagine it would go:

> *Jesus*: I have compassion for these people; they have been with me three days and have nothing to eat. I do not want to send them away hungry, or they may collapse on the way. (Jesus stares at the Twelve.)
>
> [silence] (Jesus still staring.)
>
> [silence] (Disciples stare back.)
>
> *Crickets*: chirp, chirp, chirp.
>
> [more silence, more staring]
>
> (Peter rolls his eyes.)
>
> *James* (finally blurting out): You have *got* to be kidding me!

The disciples were incredulous. Did Jesus forget they were in the wilderness? There were no options—no food, no place to get food. Obviously they needed to disperse the crowd immediately and hope for the best. The disciples never considered the possibility that help stood in their midst.

Why are we so quick to make peace with our hunger? Why did the disciples so willingly accept drought as the only viable possibility? Undeterred by the disciples' sharp cynicism, Jesus probed further, *How much bread do you have?*

At face value Jesus' question was ludicrous. The disciples' reply, whatever it might be, would make no difference whatsoever in the situation. Any response would be laughable. Whether they had no loaves or a thousand loaves, any amount would be useless with the sheer volume of people. It would be like asking how many piggy banks could have been scrounged together to finance New Orleans' post-Katrina reconstruction. Whatever the reply, Jesus knew the answer: not enough.

Nowhere close to enough.

The disciples told Jesus they had nothing to offer, only seven loaves to their name. To accentuate the desperate situation, they added unsolicited information. Often exasperated people tell you more than you care to know. "And if you want an inventory of fish too," they added, "we have only a few of those." They didn't even bother with a precise number. What did it matter?

Obviously the disciples were aware of the need for food and of their inability to effect a remedy. In fact, the disciples assumed they were more aware of the predicament than Jesus was. They may have thought their compassion surpassed that of Jesus. *Why is Jesus wasting time with these silly questions? They need food, and we have none to offer. Let's move on. The faster, the better.*

Their appraisal provided frank and plainspoken realism, but it also signaled a certain distance from the human deprivation pressing all around them. Is this how we learn to manage in a world full of grief and inequality? When we have no joy or justice to offer, must we look away, telling ourselves matter-of-factly that there is simply no way to help?

My family sponsors a child in an AIDS-ravaged country. We give through an organization that mails out regular fundraising appeals, publishing bleak global crises in bold letters across the front of the envelopes. I'm a little embarrassed to admit how rarely I open them. There are probably multiple reasons why I toss the letters, but one reason might be that it is just too overwhelming. It is easier to keep the misery at a distance than to let it up close where I must live aware of the pain and of my inability to truly change it.

If we peer closely enough, won't we see that this entire world is in a famine? Whether we are an African villager desperate for seed and rain or an East Coast urbanite desperate for companionship or a cure, we breathe in a world besieged by famine, a world God never intended. The land is hard. Love is hard. We sweat. We till the soil. Ever since our rebellion pushed us out of Eden, nothing has come easy. Nothing. Oh sure, we have our moments of bliss, but don't they seem insignificant in light of all the blight and crisis and need in the world?

The disciples, with their literalist audit of the situation, were managing the chaos by administrating. Gather data. Evaluate liabilities. Determine a course of action. Like them, we fling ourselves into smaller, more manageable stories with hopes of pushing the tumult away. If we can manhandle our academic track or romance or spiritual formation, we avoid paying attention to the many places where our lives are in dire straits. We work our jobs and devote ourselves to our kids and maneuver our friendships and constantly judge ourselves in the mirror, all in a distressed attempt to scratch our way out of the misery. Still, there is famine. Everywhere.

I actually respect the disciples' frank acknowledgment that they didn't have food to give the crowd. I am so addicted to self-reliance that if Jesus had asked me how much bread I had, I would have been tempted to shrug my shoulders as if it were no big deal and lie: "Ahh, plenty."

Growing up, I was the good son, sometimes obsessively good. While in elementary school, I once confessed with contrite anguish to my parents that I had used foul, vile language. Trying to impress an older kid, I had uttered a heinous word: *upchuck*. Could God ever forgive me?

I look back and see how I have lived much of my life believing that I could somehow prove and sustain my virtue. Over the years my sin has grown more complex. My overwrought confession has lost its effectiveness. When afflicted with guilt or inadequacy, I revert to an obsessive-compulsive path of penance, hoping again to feel good about myself. This well-worn course tells a truth: I don't believe I need the cross. I don't believe I'm a feeble sinner in need of redemption. Self-righteous religion has regularly been my preferred system for maintaining the illusion that I actually have lots of bread and plenty of fish, thank you very much.

Whatever our chosen method, we attempt to manage our stymied hopes and desires, propping up the delusion that we can somehow make good on our own. Ultimately, however, it never works. We can never scavenge or stash enough. We can never *be* enough. Novelist Toni Morrison noted our frustrating predicament: "How exquisitely human was the wish for permanent happiness, and how thin human imagination became trying to achieve it."

What do we have to show for our relentless activity, our numb inertia? What enduring nourishment have we received from our addictions, sexual dalliances, and empty piety? We are clawing after crumbs. We have scraped and scraped to produce a puny mound of loaves and fishes.

Jesus moved deftly from a broad assertion about the vast crowd's meager provisions to a particular question posed to particular individuals. "I know the mammoth throng and the enormous need, but how much bread do you have?" Jesus was not gathering data for a statistical assessment of the situation. He wondered if the disciples had wrestled with their own suffering. Had they allowed the harsh reality, the specter of mass starvation, to weigh on them with its full force? Had they given even a moment's thought to the possibility that the hunger could be alleviated? Had they considered that it wasn't only the crowd but they who were destitute?

We must listen to our hunger long enough to hear the truths it will tell us. We were not meant to live with constant emptiness. There is no shame in wanting more. Jesus had already declared his desire for the hunger to be banished. Who would join him in this declaration? Jesus was prodding the disciples toward a spark of hope or childlike wonder, toward a little curiosity about what God might have in mind.

Jesus gathered the small pile of food, the pile that was all they could pull together, all they could make of their mess. How inconsequential did that pile look, how pitiful? The act of holding seven rolls and a few limp sardines in front of the undernourished throng provided the stark, visual message: we have done our best, and famine is all we have to show for it.

I find comfort in the humanity and simplicity of Jesus' concern. The people didn't need another sermon or a prudent parable. They needed food, something they could actually sink their teeth into. There is a time to stand on the hillside and proclaim the kingdom, and there is a time to stop talking and pass out bread.

While most of us have plenty to eat, our needs are often immediate, physical. Our anxieties and wounds do not exist in theory. They are here, now. Our marriage teeters on the brink. Our father slices us with his words or silence. Our children hurt themselves incessantly. We need a Jesus who sees how hungry we are, and we need a Jesus who will care enough about us to do something about it.

Jesus seems the one most aware of and concerned by the swelling scarcity. It was not a disciple or a member of the hungry crowd who first presented the quandary of what to do with the looming crisis. It was Jesus.

Further, with the dilemma out in the open, only Jesus possessed the imagination to consider any outrageous solution. The disciples had seen Jesus raise corpses and cleanse lepers and cast a herd of demons into a herd of swine. Even more ironic, if this account is separate from the miraculous feeding of an even larger crowd just a few days before, the disciples had already seen Jesus work a miracle to answer the same quandary. Theologian Frederick Bruner says that here Matthew teaches a "doctrine of Christian amnesia." In a crisis we seldom remember the many ways God's grace has flowed toward us. The disciples' only inclination was to organize a quick exit, hoping to minimize the damage. Jesus, on the other hand, intended to arrange a feast.

God knows our pain better than we do. He sees our calamity and feels, with even greater awareness than we, how near we are to ruin. The Gospel narrative is the unfolding of a rescue operation, for those of us unaware of how much we need it and naive in the face of our complete dissolution. Like a couple lounging in their beach house, sipping cocktails as a class five hurricane barrels toward shore, we are oblivious to the peril of our situation, mistaking all the bluster as only passing winds and a feisty spring shower. In truth, our world is cracking apart, but God knows. God has come to rescue us.

Unwilling to leave the crowd famished any longer, Jesus took the bread and blessed it. Then he instructed the disciples to pass the fish and bread among them. Everyone ate, people seated in rows that seemed to go for miles. They ate and they ate and they ate some more. Mark's concluding one-word description of the crowd is beautiful: *satisfied*. The craving, for once, disappeared. God had fed them.

While the food shortage was at the front of God's immediate concern for the crowd, much more seems to be happening in the story. The crowd's physical hunger stemmed from their voracious appetite for Jesus' teaching, so starved to hear him that they followed him into the wilderness, giving no thought to their physical need for food and drink. As much as they all needed fish and bread, they were even hungrier for Jesus' strange words. All the bread in the world would not satisfy the depth of their hunger.

Further, Matthew is a theological writer, not a mere biographer. He uses the miraculous feeding as the final narrative in a trilogy woven together from conversations Jesus had with an assortment of people around the subject of food. In the first story, the religious elite were mired in pedantic detail about how one should eat, crushing the joy of a shared meal with narrow, rigid regulations. In the second story, Jesus confronted a culture that hoarded food, refusing sustenance (and friendship and mercy) to the outsider and the oppressed. In this third story, Jesus shattered the injustices brought to light in the first two encounters by providing an abundant banquet for as many as would come, particularly those who were purposefully excluded in the first two encounters: the outcasts and the marginalized. Matthew wants to make sure we know that "the lame, the blind, the crippled, the mute" were Jesus' guests at the feast. Taken together, the three stories contrast our world's chronic hunger and hoarding with the lavish, raucous feast offered in the kingdom of God.

Holy Curiosity

Jesus' miraculous banquet was not a pretext for some other purpose. Bread they needed, and bread they would get. However, in these stories, the physical (and very real) need for food played a dual, symbolic role. Jesus fed the crowd's empty bellies, but he also intended to nourish their starved souls. Elsewhere, Jesus said plainly that he was the "bread of life," the "true bread."

Jesus steadily asserted that our most profound hunger and thirst, the cravings that exert a compulsive influence over the person we become and the life we pursue and the dreams we clutch, can only be satisfied by eating and drinking him. During his ministry, Jesus poked and prodded at base human longings, suggesting that, properly recognized, they all point to God.

We are hungry for God to enter into our turmoil with us. Even more than the bread, what the crowd in the wilderness most craved were the hands that broke it. Even more than the fish, what they most desired was the God who offered it to them.

Sometimes, though, we need help remembering what we are most famished for. Often we need to actually experience a bit of famine to remember what we need. We must actually feel the hunger. Perhaps this is the reason, "[a]ccording to Jesus, when we draw near to the kingdom, it is better to come empty than full." For Jesus (unlike the disciples), hunger was an opportunity, not a predicament. The disciples didn't get it. The crowd's acute hunger provided Jesus the ideal opportunity to feed them, to visibly demonstrate that he was their provision, that he was the one they most desired and craved.

We are familiar with this impulse. Isn't one of parenting's joys the experience of guiding our children into their undiscovered pleasures? We get to introduce new delights to them. We order for them their first root beer float or take them outside after bedtime to show them their first full moon. Children don't know what they are missing until we nurture their discovery.

Recently our family trekked north to Toronto, Canada. A friend told us that we had to find a small Mediterranean diner called Mystic Muffin located in one of the downtown districts. Elias Makhoul migrated from Lebanon and opened this small dive known for the falafel, the hummus, the apple cake, and the witty remarks scribbled on the chalkboard menus. The apple cake is Elias's passion, and our friend raved about this cake. The day we went, Elias had a story sketched in chalk explaining how his love for his new country provided the inspiration for his legendary dessert. It was for love that he baked.

Elias took my order and picked up right away that we were a long way from home. As an act of hospitality, he slid a fresh piece of apple cake my way, on the house. Even with the hype, I was unprepared for the flavor party that erupted in my mouth. I'm an amateur connoisseur of apple desserts and have tasted fine culinary work, but this was beyond magnificent. Wyatt, who was five years old and considered most unfamiliar foods mortal enemies, sat next to me, and I immediately began the sales job. "You have got to try this. This is amazing. Come on, just one taste—you will freak out, it's so good!" He was uninterested. I only wanted him to take one bite, to experience the pleasure that would come from having his dormant hunger awakened and then satisfied. Wyatt never took a taste. The pita bread and Sprite had assuaged his hunger, and he was disinterested in trying anything new. Wyatt missed out. If only he had been a bit hungrier . . .

Soon after the miraculous feeding, Jesus continued to feast with the disciples. Arriving in Jerusalem and sequestering the Twelve in an upper room, Jesus passed around bread and then passed around a cup. "Eat," he said. "Drink." The hillside and upper room feedings are intricately connected. Both were preparatory acts before Jesus surrendered to Golgotha, and both had overtones of Passover, the annual celebration of God's miraculous physical provision for Israel during their exodus from Egypt. One commentator has even referred to the miraculous feeding as a second Lord's Supper. The upper room offered the Jewish version, and the wilderness hillside offered the Gentile version. It is as though Jesus wanted to emphasize that everyone is included in his feast, every nationality, every tongue and tribe, just as all were invited to the earlier hillside feast.

Jesus could have done many things with his disciples in his final hours before the torture of the cross. He could have preached a sermon, pondered the Torah, fortified strategies for the fledgling movement his followers would soon lead. But Jesus shared a meal.

Jesus has been sharing a meal ever since.

From the earliest days of God's community, the Lord's Table has held central importance in public worship. In the early church the community gathered, prayed, considered the apostles' teaching, meditated, and sang, using ancient psalms and newly created hymns—and they ate. They always distributed bread and wine, but on occasion they shared a full-on feast. These feasts were far less modest than the petite morsels and dainty sips that are part of our eucharistic celebrations. The feel would have been more like the southern potlucks of my youth, where everyone in the church was encouraged to bring an entire Sunday dinner, enough "for your entire family plus one more." At those meals, the serving tables bowed under the weight of food, and you felt absolutely miserable afterward because you hadn't paused to listen when your stomach screamed for mercy.

This generous hospitality embodies the spirit of Jesus. We find this spirit on that hillside as a man hands a basket to another man, as a mother gives bread to her children, as the people laugh and eat and have their fill. Hear their laughing. It is the noise of hospitality, the music of Christ's body.

We find this spirit in the upper room and on a cross bearing the ripped flesh and spilled-out blood. And now, every Sunday, in cathedrals and houses, in city centers and remote villages, in countless native tongues, God's people gather for a feast. We are starving, but Jesus will fill us. Let us laugh and eat and have our fill.

In our church, deacons hold the bread and wine, and we come forward. As we receive the bread, we hear echoes of Jesus' own words: "This is Christ's body, broken for you." As we dip our bread into the cup, we hear: "This is Christ's blood,

Holy Curiosity

spilled for you." Sometimes I find the experience emotive; sometimes I don't. Some Sundays the moment is somber; some Sundays it is celebratory. Sometimes, unfortunately, I just mindlessly grab bread and give it a dip. However I come, though, I'm starving. If Jesus doesn't feed me, I will die.

God has regularly met his physical creation in physical ways, appearing in dreams and on mountaintops and speaking through prophets and donkeys. God has often worked through tactile imagery, with lambs and blood and rainbows and a bronze serpent on a staff. Martin Luther liked to say God could reveal himself in every physical element, "in stone, or fire, or water, or even in a rope." At Jesus' sacramental table, I taste grace and I drink mercy. We need these physical encounters and physical reminders. "Faith needs to keep pinching itself."

I do not fully understand what Jesus meant when he passed around the bread and said it was his body. I only know this: I'm hungry. I'm lonely. I'm sinful and thirsty. The more I listen to the gospel, the more I awake to my ravenous hunger. All my gorging will never fill me, not my fantasies or my successes or my self-righteousness, no matter how furiously I stuff them down my throat. For all my hoarding, I'm exhausted, and I'm still starved. I now see the most basic truth: I'm hungry for God.

This is what I crave—a God who will pierce through history, land in the very middle of my famine, and say, with pierced hands stretched wide: "Here are some loaves and fishes, some bread and wine. Eat. Drink. Feast."

5

Are You Being Willfully Stupid?

Open to God's Surprises

"And have you no fear," said Ransom, "that it will ever be hard to turn your heart from the thing you wanted to the thing Maleldil sends?"

C. S. Lewis

We do not allow the use of the word *stupid* in our home. This word can falsely name and crush the soul. We want none of that. If our sons let it slip, particularly against each other, they land swiftly in time-out. Of course this means the word becomes the forbidden fruit, triggering all kinds of mischievous attempts to see what they can get away with. Recently one of our boys couldn't resist. Wyatt hatched a plan that he thought provided his best chance at avoiding censure. With a wily grin, he cautiously offered, "The devil . . . is stupid." Hard to argue with that.

In our contemporary experience, *stupid* demeans a person. We use the word to cut someone down or put people in their place or remind them that they are not as smart as the rest of us. These crude associations explain my surprise to hear Jesus utter the word, particularly when aimed at his disciples. Jesus had baffled the Twelve with a parable conveying the error of basing righteousness on external rites and prohibitions, particularly narrowing in on the folly of presuming certain foods to be a source of defilement. The disciples were perplexed, however, and when they got Jesus alone, they expressed their puzzlement. Jesus responded with thick irritation. *Are you being willfully stupid?* he asked.

Are we uneasy with Jesus' chafing at the disciples' ignorance? Was Jesus impatient? Did he easily fly off the handle at those unable to keep up, like the fourth-grade teacher who can't take another day with that one poke-along student who can't remember his lunch, much less his multiplication tables? I have an insecure friend who fundamentally believes she is incompetent, worthless, and fully deserving of whatever shame life can pour on her. I wince when I think of how she would hear Jesus' question. "I know, I know," she would say, her head and heart drooping low, "I *am* stupid."

As we might suspect, however, in this context, *stupid* does not imply a degrading insult. Most translations soften the blow, suggesting that Jesus asked if the disciples were "dull" or if they didn't "understand." We misread the text if we interpret this as Jesus being put off by subpar intelligence. First, we find no suggestion that the disciples were saddled with a dim wit that had finally gotten under Jesus' skin. In fact, the disciples comprehended more than many of the Jewish intellectual elite. Further, even if the disciples did possess deficient aptitude, Mark had earlier commented on how Jesus took great care to pull the disciples aside to explain to them all the mysteries his parables offered. Repeatedly in the Gospels, Jesus slowed down to make sure all who wanted to hear were provided plenty of opportunity. If Jesus' irritation had nothing to do with his short-fused patience or with the disciples' mental liabilities, then what *did* Jesus mean?

We find a measure of clarity when Jesus, rather than pausing for the disciples' reply, immediately poked the disciples further with yet another question. "Don't you see?" asked Jesus. The question's exasperated tone divulges that Jesus believed an obvious truth was parading in front of them, jumping up and down, wearing bright neon colors, just begging to be noticed; but the disciples were intent on looking away. For Jesus, stupidity is not equated with our sluggish intellectual agility. Stupidity is attached to our stubborn refusal to look up and see. Viewing the discussion in the whole, we discover that the focus of Jesus' initial harsh question was not on stupidity at all but rather on *willfulness*, the disciples' dogged refusal to open their eyes.

I identify with the disciples. There are lots of things I choose not to see. I need to lose weight. The evidence stares back at me every time I look in the mirror. It's uncanny how easy it can be to simply not look (really look) in a mirror, even when one faces me square. Often I choose not to see my stubbornness, my arrogance, my selfishness. I could take a long hard look at myself and come clean, but it's easier to look away.

Here, the disciples were flatly unwilling to take a fresh look at Jesus' words. The problem was not his obfuscatory message. In this instance (admittedly, unlike several others), Jesus' teaching was not disguised or complex. In fact, Jesus expected the gathered crowd to grasp what he was saying. "Listen to me, everyone," Jesus said, "and understand this." If Jesus expected the uninformed crowd to comprehend his teaching, no wonder he was exasperated when his closest companions pulled him aside, scratching their heads, without a clue.

While Jesus' teaching was not complicated, it was undoubtedly inflammatory and entirely unanticipated. On this occasion, with one grand swipe, Jesus overturned centuries of Jewish religious tradition and, more important, reams of Scripture's dietary restrictions. Any flippant judgment of the disciples for missing Jesus' plain teaching ought to be tempered when we remember that the disciples' eyes and ears were closed to Jesus' words on good grounds. Jesus was contradicting whole sections of Levitical code. The disciples' confusion over Jesus' teaching wasn't because the message was unclear—they simply couldn't believe the words they were hearing. Certainly Jesus did not really intend to say that no kind of food was unclean. God considered the act of consuming any form of animal's blood so egregious that any Israelite who did so was to be "cut off" from their tribe.

The Israelites had been rigidly instructed not to eat any beast that chewed the cud or had a divided hoof. To clarify, if an animal had a divided hoof but did *not* chew the cud (or conversely, if an animal did chew the cud but did *not* have a divided hoof)—those beasts were cleared for consumption. But even there, caution was required—camels and hyraxes and rabbits and pigs were off-limits. When it came to seafood, God had declared they could eat any creature that had fins and scales; but if no fins and scales, they were to abstain. With birds, most were edible, but vultures or eagles or owls or hawks or ospreys—no. Thankfully, most insects were off limits. However, if the bug happened to fly and also possessed jointed legs to help them hop (crickets, grasshopper, locusts), the Israelites were encouraged to chow down.

How could Jesus actually mean to say no food would make them unclean? God had taken deliberate care to say just the opposite. Do we have any space for a God who says one thing in one instance and on another occasion says something quite different? We are often obsessed with codifying God, insisting what he will *always* do and what he will, no matter the circumstance, *never* do. Jesus' words messed with the disciples' equilibrium. The boundaries had been well defined. They knew what God expected and how to meet those expectations. They had precise instructions for the way to order their life—no surprises, no curve balls. The codes were restrictive, but they provided a sense of continuity and safety.

However, God has never felt much of a burden to uphold symmetry or maintain safety. God's concern is far larger than keeping us comfortable. God is not patching up the old; he is radically re-creating something new, something unimagined, something wildly beautiful. In Jesus, God planted two solid, heavy feet on earth's fragile, teetering frame, the impact reverberating to every corner of our world—life piercing into death, hope overwhelming despair. In Jesus, the new creation has come.

So here Jesus stood in front of the disciples, the Son of God in plain view, declaring a new kingdom, a new community, a new day. But the disciples could not see the new because they were entrenched in the old, even though the old was never intended to be the final word, God speaking once and for all, never to speak again. The dietary restrictions and the rites of purification and the sacrificial system God had generously given to Israel's fathers and mothers were only one act in the story. Even then, the point had never been the laws and codes and restrictions. The point had always been to establish patterns and communal practices that would reveal God to them. Now, however, God was revealing himself in a dramatic new expression, thickening the plot, pushing it toward its hopeful conclusion. But the disciples would not see it, would not have it, because the old forms, the previous narratives, had overwhelmed their imagination.

Ensconced pious convention had declared that the full story was already written. The plot was already defined. The characters were set, with no room for surprises, no room for departure from the tight script. This posture squashes the mystery from any experience, whether a narrative, a marriage, or a friendship. Part of being human is discovery, being open to the fresh life always possible just around the bend.

Given this, the disciples were bound to be knocked off-kilter. When God speaks, he seeds life and unveils truth. God shows us how we've lurched off course and how we can find our way back home. But when he speaks, he never reveals all he knows. God's conversations usually leave us with a good dose of mystery.

To be truthful, the act of writing requires the writer to surrender the safe, the known, the previously mapped out. A writer must be open to what the process reveals, to the strange twists and turns that take him or her off guard. We might have a map of where we plan to head, but the map must not define the entire journey before we've even broken a sweat. Author Annie Dillard warns writers that slavishly locking in on a predetermined route can be a fatal mistake. Sometimes, she says, "[w]hat you had planned will not do. If you pursue your present course, the book will explode or collapse." This truth causes me much consternation. When I am preparing to write, I often have a cherished idea firm in my head, a story or a flow or a conclusion. There might be a phrase I want to turn or an intriguing tale I want to share. And then, just as often, after I've typed away, the sentences are listless, words flopped on a page like an old hound under the summer heat. I have a choice to make. Do I stubbornly insist on where I wanted to take the words, or do I let loose and allow the words to carry me someplace new?

If I choose poorly and remain in that marooned, myopic place, I am not open to new truth, new discovery, a radical new creation. Rainer Rilke pushes against this, instructing us that "everything, the unprecedented also, needs to be accepted. That is basically the only case of courage required of us: to be courageous in the face of the strangest, the most whimsical and unexplainable thing that we could encounter." Whenever I clamp down on what I am certain God must do, I refuse to accept—to see—the new thing God actually *is* doing.

When Miska and I were preparing for our first child, trepidation accompanied the eagerness. We had been married almost five years, and we had a good thing going. We were intimate and close. We talked about everything. We had the freedom of spur-of-the-moment weekend trips and leisurely, sleepy Saturday mornings. Aware all this was about to change, Miska wrote in her journal of our need to surrender the good that had been for the good that was coming. Last week that same child entered kindergarten, his first backpack and lunch box slung over his shoulder. Seeing him walk off to his classroom, looking back and telling us, "Don't watch me," we knew again that we must surrender the good that has been to receive the good that is coming.

Life consists of serially letting go. Even as we fully give ourselves to enjoy what we have, we must hold it loosely, always open to what will come. Unfortunately, the disciples had no plans to release any of their expectations. They held life as they knew it with a death grip.

The disciples resisted Jesus' surprising message not only because his teaching contradicted what Scripture said, but also because he contradicted what many presumed Scripture said. Jesus' way ran up against a massive configuration of Jewish religious tradition that had grown out of (and on top of) the Mosaic code. The immediate issue prompting Jesus' declaration that food could not defile a person was his anger over how the religious powers negated God's clear instructions for human compassion and justice, with their mushrooming, cumbersome web of religious tradition.

Does it surprise us to discover that Scripture can be a tool we use against God and against each other? God's revelation can be a dangerous device when the wrong person goes waving it around. Harper Lee saw this peril firsthand. In *To Kill a Mockingbird*, her character Miss Maudie voiced her experience: "Miss Maudie stopped rocking, and her voice hardened. 'You are too young to understand it,' she said, 'but sometimes the Bible in the hand of one man is worse than a whiskey bottle in the hand of [another].'"

Spiritual tradition is a double-edged sword. Used properly, it allows those who have gone before us to instruct us with their wisdom. Tradition allows us to hear the ways God's story has echoed in every generation. We have a rich heritage, and we are most foolish if we do not pay close attention. Used improperly, however, tradition is no longer a friend to instruct and guide us, but it becomes a means we use to dig in our heels, to hold on to an identity that provides us with a sense of security from a world or a God whose mystery frightens us.

I recently read *Salvation on Sand Mountain*, Dennis Covington's tale of the religious snake-handling culture in southern Appalachia. Covington, an acclaimed novelist living in Birmingham, Alabama, covered regional stories for the *New York Times* when Glenn Summerford was convicted for the attempted murder of his wife Darlene in rural Scottsboro, Alabama. Summerford was the snake-handling preacher of the Church of Jesus Christ with Signs Following (I kid you not), and he tried to kill his wife by sticking a gun to her head and forcing her to shove her hand in the crate of venomous rattlers he kept in his back shed. Bitten multiple times, Darlene survived only because Glenn passed out in a drunken stupor, allowing her to stumble her way to a neighbor's house for help.

The trial pulled Covington into this underbelly of the religious world, and he spent a year or two immersed in this strange, religious, snake-handling culture. Reading Mark 16:17–18 literally, snake-handling churches believe they should "take up serpents" as necessary signs that they are truly united with the Holy Spirit.

Curious to discover what fed this religious fervor, Covington peered into the culture's sociological history and its fascinating characters, like mythical snake handler Punkin Brown. Snake handling emerged out of a strict, experience-driven Pentecostalism. However, Covington observed that snake handling popped up only in particular environments, only where older religious cultures were encroached on by younger cultures. Deeper into the mountains, where the older culture was unthreatened, snake-handling churches were difficult to find. In urban settings where the younger cultures were firmly established, snake-handling churches were nonexistent. It was in the borderlands, where the older culture was gasping for breath, struggling to keep its footing and not be swept away, that these more outrageous religious expressions manifested. Faced with the frightening prospect of having their reality undone, they dug in, even to radical extremes. Even when church members were bitten or killed, they did not question the tradition. Lethal as it was, their tradition was familiar, something they felt a measure of control over. The handlers preferred the rattler they understood over a future they didn't.

Truthfully, my world isn't that different. I remember a man in my church when I was growing up who was angry because an African American received baptism. "They don't have a soul," he said. I was too young to remember exactly how he tangled up Scripture, but he twisted hard. I remember an evangelist who spit Bible verses as if they were sulfur belching up from his belly. He was an angry man, and he spewed angry words. His words were hard to shrug off, though, because they always were attached to "God said . . ." Neither of these men was a bad person. They were just frightened men holding on to a safe world they had carved out for themselves, a place they knew and understood. And they had found a powerful weapon to guard their terrain: Scripture.

I admit I use the same weapon. I migrate to the texts I like but conveniently gloss over the ones that make me uncomfortable. I enjoy the promises of God's blessing, but I tense up at any suggestion that I should give up anything for the sake of the poor. I migrate to the passages that fit a progressive agenda or disparage rigid sectarian spirituality, but I efficiently ignore passages that suggest God's restrictive claim on my life or behavior.

My selective (abusive) use of God and his words comes, in large part, from my acute distrust. I do not believe God's heart overflows toward me with goodness. I hold on to my small existence because I fear that if I were to surrender what I have to God, I just can't know what he will do. If I have cobbled together a spiritual regimen or a theological system or a code of discipline that defines clearly for me who I am—and how God will operate—then that affords me the benefit of order and safety. And most of us will fight and claw and use whatever tool we can grab—even the Bible—to hold on to what feels secure.

Like me, the disciples clung to safety. As a result, the disciples refused to see the new thing Jesus was doing. It was not the whores or the pagans, the spiritual outsiders flagrantly flouting God's law, who ran the risk of stupid behavior. It was the insiders, the ones who were convinced they had the answers and supposed they knew precisely what God would and would not do, to whom Jesus asked: *Are you being willfully stupid?*

And this is no trivial matter. Closing our eyes to the truth is serious business. One translation puts Jesus' question this way: "Are you so foolish?" The foolishness in mind is not the irritating but harmless sort, the kind of orneriness my Irish Uncle John McNamara calls *triflin'*. This foolishness points us back to Scripture's wisdom writers who pictured the fool as someone in grave danger, someone committed to a path that would ultimately lead to death. In the biblical sense, foolishness—stupidity—is not merely benign ignorance. It doesn't refer to sophomoric behavior, like when I work out at the gym in my "I Loved on Cholesterol All Night Long" T-shirt. Willful foolishness places me in jeopardy because I am closing my eyes and ears to my only hope, God.

One of my dearest friends has been through hell in the past year. A successful, warmhearted leader who has always deeply loved being with people, my friend can now barely leave his house. A panic attack greets him most every morning, and agoraphobia has caused him to run out of a grocery store more than once. The attacks carry such a violent, crippling power that my friend, though young and normally vibrant and healthy, at times has to use a cane to stand up straight. Midconversation, convulsions can hit. He stutters and shakes, and he has to focus all his energy to push out a single word. If I were he, I might curl up in a fetal position and waste away, but my courageous friend is doing the exact opposite.

My friend believes (and I do too) that in all this pain, somehow God is at work. While God did not cause his horror, God is using this nightmare to heal some dark and horrendous parts of his story. Recently my friend got a tattoo. Drawn from the story of Jesus washing Peter's feet, he designed a picture of a dirty, bruised, and bleeding foot, being generously washed by two strong, kind hands. He had the tattoo inked into the inside of his right forearm, a painful place to have needles piercing. He wanted it there because he would be able to see it whenever he prayed, arms outstretched and palms up. He also wanted the tattoo there because it would hurt. "I am marked by Christ," he says.

This mental and physical anguish was unexpected. My friend could turn away and refuse to see what strange, new thing God is doing. But hope and courage and faith in Jesus compel him to open his eyes to the new, unanticipated joy God might be working, the kind of joy C. S. Lewis called "a delight with terror in it."

I wonder if I will have the kind of faith my friend has, the courage to look up and see. Or will I do the foolish, stupid thing and choose to close my eyes?

> Earth's crammed with heaven
> And every common bush afire with God;
> But only he who sees takes off his shoes,
> The rest sit round it and pluck blackberries.
>
> *Elizabeth Barrett Browning*

Holy Curiosity

6

My God, Why Have You Abandoned Me?

Embracing Violent Prayer

As being man, therefore, [Jesus] doubts . . . [Jesus] speaks, bearing with him my terrors.

Ambrose

The Psalms are an assurance to us that when we pray and worship, we are not expected to censure or deny the deepness of our own human pilgrimage.

Walter Brueggemann

Recently I sat among a small circle of friends as we shared intimate pains and loneliness. The conversation was honest, compelling. While everyone listened intently, it surprised me how quickly some wanted to move the conversation past this raw place. "We have to be careful not to wallow in self-pity," one cautioned. "I'm starting to feel like I'm whining," said another. The timing was all off. We had only begun to move into honesty, only begun to explore together the places where our souls were pricked and wounded. This was the place to dig deeper, not to take a detour elsewhere, fearful we might pay too much attention to our affliction. Why are we so uncomfortable with giving ample space to sit with our sorrow?

Holy Curiosity

In another conversation, a friend's disappointment and hurt lay right on the surface. It took only a simple question (How are you doing?) for her to fling open the floodgate and let her pent-up heartache over several relational wounds gush out. After a few intense moments, however, she abruptly shifted gears, like a compass needle bolting north. She switched on a short smile and tacked on the ubiquitous line: "But . . . it's all good."

"Really?" I said. "It doesn't sound all good."

I suspect my friend believed her soul baring was too much for me. I suspect my friend believes there are fresh wounds and uneasy questions that are too uncomfortable to be offered as they are. Most of us feel that some hard words and some dark emotions should not be spoken without addendum, without softening the blow.

Jesus would disagree. Jesus spoke the darkest words. Jesus posed the bleakest question: *My God, my God, why have you abandoned me?* Jesus uttered these dire words and then Jesus dropped his head in silence.

Most of us in this emotionally enlightened age are relatively comfortable with honest expressions, in their place and as long as we are quick to remember that there are other truths. With Jesus, however, there was no follow-up, no "but . . ." The way the Gospel writer Mark narrated the story, these are Jesus' final words on the cross. All that was left for Jesus to do was die. "With a loud cry, Jesus breathed his last."

Abandoned, forgotten, left alone to die. Certainly this despair cannot be Jesus' final word. The implications make us queasy, and we scramble to find a way around them. One bothered exegete has stretched so far as to conclude that Jesus' Aramaic must have been mistranslated, suggesting that Jesus actually asked God why God had "praised" him. It is easy to understand our squeamishness. Jesus' question was brutal. "Why have you left me all alone?" The word Jesus used—*abandoned*—lacks any positive spin. It means to "leave in the lurch, forsake, desert." This was how Jesus described God the Father's shunning. Jesus did not back down from the question. He did not attempt to clarify further in order to guard against maligning God's character. God had abandoned Jesus. Jesus was enduring what Jürgen Moltmann called "the frightening eclipse of God." Jesus bore the full weight and judgment of humanity's sin . . . alone. And, quite literally, it hurt like hell.

I wonder why we are able to find immense redemptive hope in Jesus' physical suffering but are often uneasy with his emotional suffering. From my childhood, I remember long, gory sermons, graphically detailing the length of the thorns shoved into Jesus' scalp and listing the various gruesome shards imbedded in the Roman cat-of-nine-tails (bone and glass and jagged rock). We heard extensive descriptions of Jesus' beating and bleeding, the humiliation and the spitting and the ripping of his beard.

In odd contrast to this, I also remember sermons that jumped through exegetical hoops and exerted passionate energy to convince us that Jesus' plea in the Garden of Gethsemane ("My Father, if it is possible, may this cup be taken from me") was not really an anguished appeal for the Father to save him from the torture to come. The preacher said Jesus would never question God the Father's plan or wish for a way out. Jesus would never ask for such a thing.

We were skittish about Jesus' emotions. We knew his humanity required him to have human sensations, but they needed to stay tame, nothing too bleak or volatile. It was as if Jesus could be sad but never despondent, irritated but never full-on afraid. This shallow caricature yielded a Jesus who does not truly know my pain (all of it), a Jesus who has *not* experienced all our "weakness and testing," a Jesus who actually is *not* acquainted with all of our grief.

These flat, sterile perceptions of Jesus simply do not stand up. Jesus' heart and body were ripped apart. Jesus experienced utter aloneness and grappled with all the grim places of the soul. A Jewish skeptic, battered by his people's tragic history, said that he could only believe in a God who knew what it was like to be a Jewish child buried alive and what it was like to be a Jewish mother watching her suffocating child struggle for final breaths. Jesus knows these kinds of evils. In fact, Chesterton suggested that it was only in Jesus, at this bleak hour, that the most angry or despondent among us would find the "one divinity who ever uttered their isolation [and the] only . . . religion in which God seemed for an instant to be an atheist."

Contemplating Jesus' bold, frank expression highlights the discontinuity between Jesus' spiritual integrity and our own. Even though his example was to ruthlessly uncover his pain and to move toward God with it out in the open, we often use his story (the healing and hope and life he brings) as an excuse to short-circuit the way of the cross (the way Jesus won this healing and hope and life) in our own journey.

Sometimes we are committed to small desires—just to feel better or to ignore and cover our pain.

Soon enough, we will find that Jesus' way provides little aid toward that futile end. Jesus did not come to help us maneuver around our brokenness; Jesus came to enter our brokenness with us. The gospel is not a therapeutic system tooled for enhancing our ability to cope by believing hard enough and smiling big enough and quoting just the right mixture of Bible verses so we can distance ourselves from our negative emotions. The gospel is the story of the world as it actually is, our lives as they actually are. The gospel tells us we are broken, more broken than we know, and that our world is in shambles. Jesus does not encourage us to ignore what we have lost, but rather to mourn it, to feel deep sorrow over the devastation we were never supposed to know. The gospel instructs us to want and wait and hope for God to make the world right again. We do not need a God removed from our destruction and insisting we are all okay. We need a God who knows in his bones how sick we are and who will not leave us to ourselves. We need God to rescue us.

Hope does not lie in ignoring these truths but rather in facing the reality of our predicament. We must feel the full weight of our shattered heart; and then, splintered remnants in hand, we must turn to God for redemption. I am suspicious whenever our religion has no room to weep or mourn or be angry. I am suspicious when we move too quickly past our pain. The point, of course, is not to wallow in drab self-pity, but we cannot surrender our pain to God if we are unwilling to acknowledge it exists. To paraphrase a political bumper sticker, if we are unaware of the ruin all around us, we aren't paying attention.

Jesus did not flinch from the truth. He wept over the wreckage scattered all about him. Jesus would not mute his lament. *Why have you forsaken me?*

Though I want to hear the answer to Jesus' question, I am actually most compelled to ponder the context, what it means for Jesus to have spoken these forlorn words directly to his Father (*My God, my God*). Some of us might be comfortable unleashing our unbridled emotions with close friends, but few of us would ever be comfortable speaking these things to God. Jesus was not venting to a companion or a therapist. Jesus assaulted heaven with his perplexed agony. Jesus was praying.

And this was no off-the-cuff prayer. Jesus had been taught to pray this way. His words voiced a Jewish prayer of lament taken directly from Psalm 22. Psalms is the Jewish prayer book, actually five different books full of prayers for singing and prayers for reading all collected in one volume known as the Psalter. Among the Psalms, we find prayers expressing hope and prayers venting despair, prayers asking God to afflict enemies with judgment and prayers begging God not to forget his impoverished people. The Psalter exhibits the full range of human emotions and models for us the brave, dangerous act of bringing all these emotions directly to God. The Psalms suggest that prayer is not saying the right thing but saying the honest thing. Though the "Our Father" is properly called the Lord's Prayer, we would do well to remember another of the Lord's prayers, tucked away in a psalm that has been described as a "song of grief and abandonment."

I don't know if I could have handled a Jewish prayer gathering when the lectionary called for the more gut-wrenching collects. "God, I don't like you very much. God, I don't believe you are acting with justice in the world. God, my enemies are about to take me out; could you take them out first?—and make it hurt." Walter Wink describes biblical prayer as "impertinent, shameless, indecorous . . . more like haggling in an oriental bazaar than the polite monologues of the churches." Some of the psalmist's prayers make poor theology. The prayers aren't always correct (God is always just and kind and present, even if it doesn't appear so), but the prayers are always true (always offering frank expressions of the state of the heart). This is prayer—coming to God with all that we are, the glorious pieces as well as the sick pieces, and asking God to see us, to hear us, to enter with us into whatever mess or joy we find ourselves in.

There are many fights at our house these days. Our boys are hitting that age when *play* is too docile a word for what they do. What they engage in is more like a reenactment of the Tet Offensive. They do own Legos and Tinker Toys, but the toy rifles and medieval swords and light sabers are the crowd favorites. Recently Wyatt was full of the Dark Side and landed a particularly lethal blow on Seth with his light saber, causing Seth to scream and wail. It was pitiful. Because of several factors, it became obvious that Wyatt was using these duels to vent pent-up anger. So I sat Wyatt down for a serious talk about displaced rage and our human tendency to unleash destructive emotions on those who really are not the culprits of our subconscious turmoil.

Wyatt, you should remember, is five.

About halfway through my insightful explanation, I began to question whether Wyatt had the first clue about what I was saying. "Do you understand what I am saying?" I asked.

"Yes," Wyatt answered.

"How much of it?"

"All of it."

He was too eager to please. I was suspicious. "*Really*? Or are you just saying that because you think I want you to?"

A pause. A slow, coy smile broke across his face. "I'm just saying it."

"So, for real, how much do you understand?"

"None of it."

Many of us pray this way. We edit and parse and fastidiously search for proper, well-reasoned words. We work to pray good theology. We hide behind religious rhetoric. But we do not truly pray, not in the way Scripture teaches us to pray. We do not bare ourselves, ugliness with the beauty, faith with the doubt, eagerness with the boredom. We believe mistakenly that prayer is speaking to God what he wants to hear rather than speaking to God what is truly in us.

The prayers the Psalms teach us to pray are "not religious in the sense that they are courteous or polite or deferential. They are religious only in the sense that they are willing to speak this chaos to the very face of the Holy One." Prayer simply speaks honestly. Some prayers express honest delight and adoration and gratitude and submission and hope. Then some prayers must have other conversations with God. "No, I am not filled with love. In fact, God, I'm not sure if I trust you . . . or like you . . . or want you right now. The truth is that I am really angry." For those of us uncomfortable with acknowledging what is broken inside us, the Psalter's poem-prayers give us a vocabulary for our brokenness. And, as Walter Brueggemann says, "When we learn to pray these prayers, we shall all be scandalized."

Recently Miska and I began a discussion that became intense and frustrating. Though the conversation had grown uncomfortable and seemed fruitless, Miska's strongest frustration was when she felt me disengaging and withdrawing emotionally from her. "Don't pull away from me," she said. However, it's easier to retreat than to muck your way through all the uncertain relational tumult. What wounds Miska the most, though, is not the turmoil or my negative emotion but rather my emotional retreat. "Stay with me," she says.

I hear God's words here. Do not retreat. Do not hide your ugliness or your unpleasant emotions. I can handle them. Just don't back away. Stay with me. This is prayer.

The Psalms are a powerful tutor for prayer, not only because they teach us to be brutally honest, but also because they come to us as poems—and poetry, as any lover will tell you, provides a language for the soul. Poetry allows us to say things that other forms of expression are unable to communicate. At times, poetry even provides us the possibility to speak more than we fully comprehend. This is the reason Kathleen Norris says that "[t]he discipline of poetry teaches poets, at least, that they often have to say things they can't pretend to understand." If we pray only what we understand, then our prayers are limited to our imagination and are doomed to be as narrow as our view of what God might be doing in our world. If we pray only what we understand, our conversations with God grow small and lifeless and polite.

There is an advantage to polite prayer, though. It is safe. As we present to God our catalogued agenda or parrot back to God what we believe he wants to hear from us, we keep any unsavory emotions or potential conflict with God at a distance. Jesus' prayer, however, was little concerned with equilibrium or etiquette. His prayer was unguarded, unmeasured. I don't get the sense that Jesus ran his prayer through a theological grid to check if it was appropriate. Jesus cried out of his pain, *My God, why?*

Poetry is a contemplative art, observant and curious. Often poets muse about the simplest things, the most unobtrusive details. The poet believes that truth is often hidden among the quiet and common things. This makes poetry an essential metaphor for prayer. The Psalms, Jesus' prayer book, guide me to pay attention to my own story, to attune to the places where joy is just beginning to spark or where fear has slowly spread its seed. The praying poets of the Psalms insist I pay attention to the interior of my soul so that I know where God wants to heal and touch.

A poem's richest power is not from the lexicon it employs but from the experience it evokes. After the lines have been read and the rhythm and meter have done their work, then, in the profound silence, we are left with true poetry. That said, it should not surprise us that some of the best prayers are unspoken. They simply form in quietness, in waiting or listening. Sometimes the only prayer we have to offer is our tears. Jewish tradition taught that prayer had ten names, and the first was *cry*. Some of our truest prayers offer only a few words. Often I find myself simply praying, "Mercy, because of Jesus." Really, what more could I say?

I have a friend who believes that, at the core, there are only two prayers: *help* and *thank you*. I think this is true, but my difficulty arises in the many miles I must trudge after I say help but long before I have any reason to say thank you.

Jesus knew what it was to suffer long. He had been harassed for his entire public ministry. Now that the authorities had him, they scourged him and humiliated him and whipped him and forced him to climb Golgotha Hill carrying heavy, rough timber on his lacerated back. The guards had spit on him and nailed him to the wood, which they dropped into the ground with a jolting thud. Where was God in all of this?

Once Jesus was hoisted up on the cross, the text purposefully highlights that Jesus hung there for three hours, a miserable stretch when "darkness came over the whole land." What happened in those three dark hours? We know this: God did nothing. God was nowhere to be found. It's interesting, though, that Mark notes the precise moment when Jesus spoke. It was three o'clock, the ninth hour as the older versions put it, a traditional hour of Jewish prayer. A Hebrew reader would have heard the text this way: "And then, after three brutal hours of pain and emptiness, at the hour for prayer, Jesus cried loudly, *'My God, my God, why have you forsaken me?'* "

It would be an injustice, however, to interpret Jesus' words as expressing despair only. Jesus was *praying*, after all. He was crying out to God. Jesus felt his Father's cold absence but he believed that God was still listening, even if his experience pointed to the contrary. Jesus' prayer was the sturdiest act of faith, the faith to be brutally honest about God's inaction and, at the same time, filled with relentless trust that God's kindness would tell the final story. This is why passionate words, whenever our soul is in a severe place, are more faithful prayers than the polite lines we are tempted to offer. Our courteous, shallow prayers belie our belief that our faith will not hold up under the strain of a God who is not, in this moment, answering our questions or smoothing out our path. When we no longer feel the need to protect ourselves from the contradiction between what we expect God to do and what God actually does, when we believe in God's good heart without demanding its validation at every turn—then we are beginning to swim in faith's deep waters.

A further look at Jesus' question gives us even stronger suggestions that his words were an expression of robust faith. In Hebrew custom, one would often quote the opening lines or a memorable passage from a Scripture text to reference the entire section.

Most likely, Jesus was not only excerpting a piece from the psalm but was also invoking the entire psalm as his prayer. At first, the prayer plunges further into murkiness: "My God, I cry out by day, but you do not answer." Then along the way, we begin to hear hints of hope: "But you, Lord, do not be far from me." "Rescue me from the mouth of the lions." Next the prayer moves into outright triumph: "[God] has not despised or scorned the suffering of the afflicted one; he has not hidden his face from him but has listened to his cry for help." Finally, the prayer ends with gusto, a celebration breaks out: "Posterity will serve him; future generations will be told about the Lord. They will proclaim his righteousness, declaring to a people yet unborn: He has done it!"

When Jesus uttered his disheartened words, he was praying an entire narrative, a story that began in honest admission of bewildered abandonment but also trusted in a hopeful end, one where God had made all things right. Jesus' despairing cry was not his final word. Resurrection would trump death. This is why author Henri Nouwen could believe that "[w]here God's absence was most loudly expressed, God's presence was most profoundly revealed."

It can be no accident that the prayer Jesus evoked concluded with a resounding declaration that future generations would be submerged in God's inescapable goodness. This future redemption was precisely the reason Jesus hung on a cross, the reason why he had been abandoned. In Jesus, God abandoned himself. God's love moved him to a rescue that would cost him absolutely everything. In fact, Jesus prayed this prayer with a measure of truthfulness we cannot. Jesus was abandoned so that we would never be.

Jesus submitted himself to unthinkable horror, to the place where his only truthful prayer would be: *My God, my God, why have you forsaken me?* so that we could hear God speak starkly different words to us: "Never will I leave you; never will I forsake you."

7

Are You Confused?

The Gift of Disorientation

You don't believe my words now, but you'll come to it yourself.
. . . Suffering is a great thing.

Fyodor Dostoyevsky

God acts in mysterious ways.

Fénelon

Jesus' disciples were in a fog much of the time. On a few occasions they seemed to know what Jesus was up to. Most of the time, however, they were off in the corner scratching their heads. John narrated one of these flummoxed moments when Jesus' words, rather than resulting in clarity, flung the disciples into a tornado of confusion. His words unnerved his followers. They would be hated, he said. They would be victimized. They would be thrown out of the synagogue, the seat of Jewish political power and religious authority. Some of them would be murdered. And there was more. Even worse things would befall some of them, but mercifully Jesus said he would stop there.

Jesus did add one last thing: "In a little while you will see me no more, and then after a little while you will see me." What a strange way to talk! Why couldn't Jesus just say what he meant? The disciples whispered among themselves, throwing possible interpretations back and forth. But no interpretation worked. "What does he mean?" they asked. "We don't understand."

Then Jesus reentered the conversation. "Are you asking one another what I meant?" This was a gentler way of putting the question Jesus was really posing: *Are you confused?*

Yes, yes, they were. And why not? Jesus was talking in cryptic language. Even more befuddling, he was saying outlandish things about their being killed and losing any shot at power. What sense did that make? Jesus was going to be king. They were going to ride in on his coattails. Behind the scenes, they were already divvying up the spoils. They had gambled their businesses and their families and their futures to follow him, but it would all pay off in the end; they knew it. So, yes, Jesus, they were confused.

Most Sundays after our church's gathering, our two boys, Wyatt and Seth, like to sprint out the front doors and play in the courtyard. They like to run behind the bushes, the ones they have dubbed their secret fort, where they strategize and gather courage to fight the monsters mingling outside. They also like to peer at all the fish in the little pond, pointing out which is their favorite and tossing a rock in the water when Mom and Dad aren't paying attention. It's a small area, and it gets chaotic, bottlenecking with all the people exiting church.

One Sunday I had "boy-duty." It's usually pretty easy to keep an eye on Wyatt, but Seth, who was three at the time, is a different matter. He's quick and wily. He's stealth—on steroids. I got caught up in a conversation, and when I looked around to catch sight of the boys, I couldn't find Seth. I spoke into the bushes, asking the other kids if Seth was there. He wasn't. I looked around, but the crowd was too thick. I couldn't see him anywhere. I had one of those short, panicky moments every parent knows. I began to call out for Seth, yelling his name, with no response. I had seen a little flash of something up at the top of the courtyard area, moving toward the parking lot where lots of cars would be in a rush to get out. Seth was short; we still measured him in inches, not feet. If he ran out into a parking lot with tight traffic, no one would see him. It was only seconds, but it was plenty of time to give me that spinning, trepid disorientation. And then I saw Seth running toward me. He jumped in my arms and squeezed tight, as if he were releasing his fear onto me. "I couldn't find you," Seth said, pushing his cheek against mine. He had felt it too, the unsettling, fearful moment when our world is tilted off balance. We all know it. None of us like it.

Common and unpleasant as this off-balance confusion might be, it is particularly disturbing when it is God who provides the confusion. Like the disciples, we consider God to be the sure thing, the stable one. I have used confident terms like *faith* and *promise* to describe my sense of God. These are concrete, hefty terms. Yet what I say and what I experience don't always connect. I feel like poet Robert Lowes: "I'm having a devil of a time making faith's familiar words behave." *Confused* is a good word, a great word, to describe how we feel toward God sometimes, maybe even most of the time.

When we encounter the stark, untamed God of the Scriptures, the disorienting experience moves us off center. Often we feel the need to ease the tension or avoid the seeming contradictions or hurry to a more familiar truth. Kids' books, in particular, have a hard time with the Bible. Noah's ark is a favorite children's theme with all the cuddly animals and the cool boat ride. The pictures of the zebras and the giraffes and the little pigs walking in line onto the boat—what kid wouldn't love that? But I don't think I've ever seen pictures of the drowning victims clawing for another gasp of air as the floating zoo sails away. That would make for a more traumatic bedtime, for sure. In all our boys' Bible storybooks, I've never seen one tackle the subject of God's instructions for Israel to annihilate the Amalekites, including moms, dads, animals, children, and all. "'And then, God told his people to kill all the kids and all their furry friends. The end.' Off to bed now!"

One book we read to our boys tells the story of Jesus. When it comes to the crucifixion, it voices bewilderment over why anyone could ever have wanted to harm Jesus when he "never did hurt anyone." I can't bring myself to read that line. I usually alter the words on the fly with something less syrupy.

I'm not suggesting we unload all of Scripture's complexities on our preschoolers. I am suggesting that we are addicted to creating a version of God that is more manageable, less confusing—and our addiction is so pervasive it shows up even in the stories we tell our children. What my boys need, what I need, is a God who tells his own story, a God larger than anything I could create. Sometimes, the story God tells will take turns and go places I am unable to comprehend.

Good stories are big stories, and big stories create a new world, pulling me in. Bad stories are little stories with little plots and small, predictable characters. Little stories never confuse, but they also never create. They do not change me. They don't offer me anything I couldn't have gotten on my own.

God is not surprised by our confusion. To the contrary, he invokes it. Jesus peddles mystery. It is Jesus who tells the riddles and speaks the strange words. It is Jesus who raises the whole question about confusion—and Jesus who won't let it go. Confusion is not always a barrier to God. Often confusion is a path to God. The disciples had one interpretation, one framework, for the reality to which Jesus was calling them. Their world had to be stretched. It had to be pulled wide and hard. Confusion and disorientation did the stretching.

Jesus used hard-to-understand words and perplexing notions to unsettle his disciples. Earlier in the conversation recorded in John, Jesus was disturbed, not by their confusion, but by their lack of questions. "None of you are asking me what I am up to. Why aren't there more questions?" Jesus prodded. There is a time for answers and clarity, and then there is a time when the only appropriate state is confusion. This was a time for confusion. The Spirit who would lead them to truth would come *later*. The plan for redemption would be unfolded *later*. But now, in this moment, if they weren't at least a bit confused, if questions weren't bubbling to the surface, it was a signal that they weren't paying attention.

When the disciples finally spoke up, asking what Jesus was talking about, it was the first time John had mentioned their speaking since Judas had voiced his puzzlement about Jesus' activities a couple of chapters earlier. Between these two verbalized confusions, we find the longest running monologue John offers, the longest stretch of Jesus' speaking without other voices. But Jesus didn't want to be the only one talking. He wanted a conversation, engagement. The disciples had grown too silent, too complacent or disinterested. Their lack of questions disquieted Jesus. I've never heard a homily on the merits of confusion, but Jesus seemed on the verge of providing one here. If the disciples weren't confused, weren't wrestling with his words, something was wrong. When we are confused, at least we're part of the action. Being confused can signal that we are still vested in the relationship, that we are paying attention. I once heard it said that confusion is the height of consciousness. I don't know about that, but one thing we can be sure of when we're confused is this: at least we're not dead.

Do we really think it possible to follow the ways of God without having our world turned over? Do we really expect to follow a God we always understand, who always conforms to our expectations? Could confusion (at times) be a sign that we have actually heard God correctly? Disorientation shouldn't be disdained; it is inevitable. If the Jesus we hear never finishes a sentence differently than we imagine he would, if the Jesus we claim to follow never offers an ideology in direct contradiction to what we have grown comfortable with, if the Jesus we envision never loves people we would never expect him to embrace, we might need to revisit the Gospels. We might need to be reintroduced to the biblical Jesus.

Anne Lamott says, "You can safely assume you've created God in your own image when it turns out that God hates all the same people you do." It is a constant temptation to make God a reflection of me, rather than me a reflection of him. There ought to be a certain level of dissonance between what I expect from Jesus and what Jesus actually does. There should be some confusion.

The disciples couldn't imagine a God who would endure the kind of suffering Jesus described for himself, and they certainly couldn't imagine a God who would have them endure violence and upheaval. Can we?

When Jesus warned the disciples of the coming torments, when they would be afflicted and treated as outcasts and murdered, they had no reference point for it. Minimalist theology tempts us to believe that Jesus' primary purpose is to save us from hell, and in so doing to save us from every brush with evil and despair. But what if Jesus also came, not to keep us from hell, but to invite us into hell? What if Jesus came to invite us to enter, with him, into the terrors of brokenness and sin and misery in our world? In the scandal of the incarnation, Jesus took on human form and immersed himself in his world spun off course. On the cross, he was drenched in our sin. During his three days entombed in darkness, many traditions teach that Jesus descended into the depths of Hades to confront Satan and his hordes. If we as God's people are now called to incarnate Jesus in our world, how could we possibly think Jesus' ultimate aim is to make sure we are always comfortable, that we get our piece of the American dream?

Jesus invites us into the reality of his work, bringing redemption to the earth and speaking revolutionary Jesus-life to a dead, broken world. But when we are committed to smaller stories, wrapped up in ourselves, this will be a jolt. It will be confusing. There will be doubts. And, it seems to me, every bit of the confusion is necessary, a signal that it is actually God at work. God is up to something.

Eugene Peterson once said that, as pastors, it is not our job to make God and his world simple. Our task is not to create a fantasy reality and then try to include God in it. Our task is to bring people into God's world—as it is. And God's world—as it is—at times appears quite muddled. But how could it be any other way? Is this not a signal that we are actually grappling with God, true God, large and alive God? Is this not a signal that we are honestly coming to terms with the truth that we are not God, that we are mortals submitting to God's rule over us? Miguel de Unamuno, a Spanish writer of the early twentieth century, supposed that honest grappling was a sign of faith. "Those who believe that they believe in God, but without any passion in their heart, without anguish of mind, without uncertainty, without doubt, without an element of despair . . . believe only in the God-Idea, not in God Himself." Could confusion (at times) be a sign that we have actually heard God correctly? Could confusion (at times) be a sign that we are about to get on the right track, or a gracious warning signal that we are headed in the wrong direction and need to make a change?

It's not as though confusion is inherently good; there is no ethical plus to getting God wrong. But since we are fallen humans in a fallen world, there is much space between what we know and see and assume and what God is actually making of our world. God is not limited only to what we are able to envision. God must loosen our grip from what we presume so he can put something else before us. Disorientation is a prime way God pries away our fingers.

Distressing though it is, the pain of disorientation is indispensable. Jesus said as much. He compared the disciples' inevitable confusion to the pain of childbirth. "A woman giving birth to a child has pain," said Jesus, "because her time has come." It isn't complicated. The pain comes because it is the time for pain. Much of our lives are given to futile attempts to eradicate all pain, to keep ourselves from ever experiencing disorientation or fragmentation. We never want to feel anything less than whole. The wisdom writer of Ecclesiastes suggests this is a callow view of the world. There is a time to be healed, but there is also a time to be torn apart. There is a time to dance, but there is also a time to cry deep tears (see 3:1–8). There is a time for everything, because we need everything; we need it all.

Some dancing comes only after deep sorrow.

This is the point of all the struggle and the confusion: life. Birth is the painful, joyful process of bringing something new into the world, something that has been forming miraculously in a more hidden place. But what was hidden has to get out. It must, even though it will hurt.

And it does hurt. I've seen it firsthand. I watched Miska give birth to our first son, Wyatt. I purposefully say *watched* because I didn't do much else. Miska had determined to deliver Wyatt *au naturel*, without the aid of an epidural or any pain medication. I was inspired by her care for the young life in her tummy, and I was intrigued by her holistic approach, being in harmony with her body and this new life coming from her. But, *really*, can you imagine passing a medium-sized watermelon out of your body without so much as an aspirin?

But life came from the pain. I now have a boy, two in fact, who wrestle and laugh and drive Miska and me crazy and say the oddest things and snore like semi-trucks blowing their horns. Miska would tell you every pain was worth it. Just look at the life.

With a human birth, if you give it enough months, you can at least see visible hints of progress. With God's work in the soul, it is often entirely undercover. Given this, our quandary is that we just can't see what God is up to. What the disciples lacked, what we lack, is the discipline required to move through disorientation and on to something solid.

We also lack spiritual imagination. Spiritual imagination is the ability to see God at work, to see God engaged in places and ways we would never see otherwise. "It takes imagination to live in God's world," says N. T. Wright. It takes imagination to see how beauty might come out of suffering, and imagination to believe in Jesus' peace amid a violence-torn world. Often we just can't imagine what God might be doing, but we need to. The value of confusion is that it disorients us to our world so that we can be available to God's world. Confusion, understood this way, is entirely necessary.

The other night, I heard Wyatt talking to his brother, Seth. They share a bedroom, and there is no end to the mischief they cook up when they are supposed to be going to sleep. I couldn't hear the details, but Wyatt was trying to get Seth to do something or pretend something. Apparently Seth was protesting that it was impossible; he couldn't do it. "Use your imagination!" I heard Wyatt say. Sometimes, imagination is the only way.

Luke tells of another time the disciples were confused by Jesus' prediction of his coming death. Luke tells us that the disciples had no idea what Jesus meant by his words, but "they were afraid to ask him about it." Fear is understandable. Disorientation breeds fear. But we must go to Jesus with our fear and our uncertainty, never allowing fear to keep us at a distance.

God's ways disorient, but disorientation is not the end. Confusion opens up other possibilities. Confusion pushes us past smallness, past dead ends. All the hell into which Jesus would soon descend, all the hell Jesus invited his disciples into, was not the end.

After hell, resurrection comes.

God's purpose is not merely to befuddle us, proving he's God and rubbing our noses in the fact that we're not. All of God's intent, from the moment Adam and Eve were pushed from the Garden until the good end when he will bring us into the renewed Garden, is redemptive. God is restoring. God is making new. Between what we see and what God has to show us, however, there is a lot of death, a lot of confusion, a lot of hell.

In *Crime and Punishment*, Dostoyevsky penned a tale of disorientation that gave way to the hope of redemption. Radion Romanovitch was a Russian student who, partly as an act of justice and partly for selfish motives, murdered an old, malevolent woman. Porfiry Petrovitch was the constable intent on proving Romanovitch committed the crime. Petrovitch's voice became (unwittingly, perhaps) one of redemption, encouraging Romanovitch to do the unthinkable, to confess his transgression. Romanovitch couldn't imagine such a foolish act, but Petrovich urged that this irrational, disorienting act would bring him to another reality. "I know you don't believe in it," Petrovich said, "but . . . fling yourself straight into life, without deliberation; don't be afraid—the flood will bear you to the bank and set you safe on your feet again. What bank? How can I tell? I only believe that you have long life before you."

Romanovitch's disorientation might be different from the kind we face, but his choice whether to "fling himself into life" is a choice common to us all. The way to redemption will include confusing stretches when we must determine if we will trust what God wants to do in us. It might require suffering. It will always require humble obedience, a letting go. What does God have in mind? How can we tell? We are unable to see, as Dostoyevsky said of Romanovitch, how new life will come out of our disorientation. It will though. It will.

The passing is hard. The way is confusing. We must fling ourselves straight into it. God is working good in us. Believe it: we have a long life before us.

8

Do You Believe This?

How God's Silence Speaks

It is one of the triumphs of the human that he can know a thing and still not believe it.

John Steinbeck

O nly twenty-eight years young, Melissa barely made it past her son's second birthday before she died. Soon after Melissa gave birth to Drew, what seemed a nasty cold persisted until she went to the doctor and received the devastating news: leukemia. Her first bout, with the chemotherapy and the drugs and the exhaustion and her hair falling out, almost finished her off. But Melissa fought back courageously, and the doctors began to cross their fingers and use hopeful words like *progress* and *remission*.

Melissa had married Nathan, one of my closest friends from college. We were in each other's weddings and have seen each other through many seasons. None, however, like this. One afternoon, Nate called me with the grim news that Melissa's leukemia was back. His voice told the story— he was worn out, scared. The next few months, we traded phone calls, and I tried to be a part of the nightmare he was enduring. But it was hard—Miska and I were living in Denver, and he and Melissa were in Dallas. Nathan did have people around him, neighbors and friends from church, who were deeply involved. They cared for Drew. They brought meals. They prayed. One night there was a prayer vigil on their block, a large gathering where people held hands and created a huge circle surrounding their entire house. Friends prayed. Moms and dads prayed. I prayed.

Then Melissa died.

When I arrived in Dallas for the funeral, Nathan looked dull and empty. His heart had ripped open, and like a tub losing its last ounce down the small, gulping drain, all the hope had emptied out. His sorrow had left him numb, cold, and barren. I think some part of his soul was desperate to feel something, anything, just to laugh or cry, to know he was still human, still alive.

In moments like this, words are little help. So we did all we knew to do. Nathan, his brother, and a few of our other friends grabbed cigars and headed to a local park. We sat under the clear Texas sky and smoked and talked and hugged and prayed. What else can you do when death has arrived too soon and when your life has been ripped away?

There isn't much that will shatter our faith more than a God who goes silent while one we love suffers or while our heart surrenders to darkness, a God who is silent while our life crumbles. Where do we go when the story line turns bleak and when God doesn't do what God is supposed to do? God doesn't answer our prayer. God doesn't show up on time.

When the Gospel writer John introduces us to Lazarus, we have to wonder if there is an ill-advised attempt at sarcasm in the story. Lazarus's name means "God helps," but as the narrative unfolds, God seems more an adversary than an ally. Martha and Mary, Lazarus's sisters and Jesus' longtime friends, lived together in Bethany, a village whose name ("house of suffering") would soon prove a better etymological fit for their distraught reality. Lazarus was gravely ill, and the desperate sisters had one hope: Jesus. They had seen Jesus accomplish bewildering feats, and so they rushed off a hasty message, hoping to reach Jesus in time.

The message was short, to the point. "Lord, the one you love is sick." There was no need to plead or cajole. The sisters didn't even need to provide a name. They needed only to mention that the one Jesus loved was in need. Jesus would know who. Confident their friend would return quickly, their question was whether Lazarus could hold on long enough for Jesus to arrive.

When the messenger found Jesus, urging him to scramble back to Bethany, John offered a biographical insertion. John reminded us that Jesus loved Martha and he loved her sister, Mary, and he loved Lazarus, the one tempting death. Reading of Jesus' warm fondness for his friends, we are relieved to know how this will go. Jesus will hurriedly gather up his disciples and sprint to Lazarus's side. It will be a dramatic finish, but the story will end well. Good stories always do.

However, since John knew where the story was heading, I wonder if he felt compelled to reiterate Jesus' love, fearful we would soon think otherwise. When the frantic news reached Jesus, he did nothing . . . for two long days. Lazarus was sick; death was imminent. And Jesus sat. Jesus resumed his conversation. He ate a meal, then another and another and another, five or six in all. He slept. Jesus just waited. And while Jesus waited, Lazarus died.

It takes only a little inertia to cause devastation. God doesn't have to rain down judgment or flatten a square city mile to allow ruin to take hold. All God has to do is refuse to move, to simply stay far out of reach or refuse to speak. What good is a God who will not move when movement is what we desperately need? What good is a God who will not speak when a word is what our dire situation demands? Nothing obliterates our Pollyanna vision of God like silence and seeming apathy.

God's apparent capriciousness is all the more unbearable when we have kept our end of the bargain. This is the way it works, we're told: we do our part and God does his. We are faithful with spiritual disciplines and don't sleep around on our wife and remember to vote the way Jesus would, and God will answer our prayers and smooth out our path. We aren't so foolish as to assume God will deliver on our every whim, but we do believe that when legitimate concerns or potential calamities are in play, God will come through. He's a sure bet. Comfortable with these odds, dutifully we fulfill our end of the bargain, but tragedy still erupts. And Jesus just waits. While Jesus waits, our child's kidney transplant never arrives or our marriage can't hold on or our dad shoves a twelve-gauge into his mouth. Yet, in each case, we had hoped and prayed and begged and believed.

Often God is the contrarian. Scripture offers a scattering of helpful principles—sowing and reaping, praying and being answered, hoping and the hope coming true. Yet there is also an unruliness to God, a refusal to be tamed. God never intended for his wisdom and principles, even his promises for that matter, to be our leverage to force him into the corner we choose. We *do* have strong scriptural precedent for appealing to God's faithfulness to keep his promises, hoping to provoke God's movement. However, this bold, biblical posture models a humble faith entwined in the sinews of relationship (with all the mystery, passion, and wrestling raw relationships possess), not a manipulative tool invoked to assert power over God.

Scripture does insist on God's good heart toward his creation. God is eager to overwhelm us with generosity and kindness. However, God's lavish impulse does not diminish his wild nature. When we reduce God's revelation and liberal character to mere formulas, we expose how we want safety and control more than we want God. This will never do.

When Jesus decided it was time, he told his disciples to prepare for the trek to Bethany. Jesus' return was unhurried and deliberate. By the time he reached the edge of the city, Lazarus had been in the tomb four days. When tragedy hovers, we do not expect Jesus to linger or dawdle. However, Jesus was *intentionally* four days late.

At what point do we consider Jesus' actions cruel?

The precise number of days that John noted is a significant detail. Rabbinic tradition held that resurrection was possible for a corpse up until the third day. After that, there was no hope. Not only had Jesus' response allowed Lazarus to die, but his measured return landed him in Bethany suspiciously on the day we might call "the day *after* hope."

When Jesus arrived in the house of suffering, he found a hope-drained, grieving sister, Martha. "Why?" she asked. Jesus could have saved her brother, and he didn't. *Why?*

This question—*why?*—is central to humanity's dilemma with God. For many of us, we cannot escape the haunting notion that God is there, out there, somewhere. But he is so . . . unpredictable. If God is good, *why?* If God is love, *why?* What can we possibly pretend to know of this one named God when his movements are so erratic and his voice so quiet? Martha's aching words reveal a woman struggling to hold on even though her faith had been pounded into the ground and now seemed limp and useless. What was she to make of this Jesus who spoke God-words, who offered her love, and yet who had refused her when she needed him most?

Sorrow and angst do not frighten Jesus. Jesus' compassion for Martha ran deep, but he wanted to do something more for Martha than help her avoid her anguish. Jesus wanted to show Martha a wider vista. He deeply desired, for her good, to push the conversation in an unnatural direction. Answers might come later, but this was not the time for answers. Jesus determined to invite Martha to a reality bigger than herself, larger than her grief. Jesus—and the gospel he embodies— always calls us out of ourselves and into the larger story.

From the first moment Jesus received news of Lazarus's sickness, Jesus was moving (or refusing to move) with deliberate purpose. He was not callous or inattentive to the pain of others. Rather, he saw things that others were unable to perceive. "This sickness will not end in death," Jesus said. "It will become an occasion to show God's glory by glorifying God's Son." Jesus' words echo a portion of John's broader literary perspective. One of John's theological themes was to collect a series of dramatic signs that would serve as witness to the fact that Jesus was indeed the long-awaited Messiah sent from God to rescue his people and his world from ruin. Jesus' encounter with Lazarus was near the climax of these swelling stories of miraculous signs.

Notice Jesus' precise words. Jesus did *not* say Lazarus would not die, but that this story would not *end* in death. This story was far larger than Lazarus and Mary and Martha. Our stories, though vital and beautiful and in need of God's attention, are always substories, only one part of the larger redemptive narrative God is writing in his world. Mary and Martha did not see it yet, but their pain was not only about them. God was working for the good of all his creation. God was up to something they had not yet imagined.

Wanting Martha to catch glimpses of the bigger story, Jesus did not answer Martha's *why*. He did not dismiss her question, nor did he respond directly. Jesus had something more important to say: "I am the resurrection and the life."

Life. Resurrection. These were the very things Martha had begged Jesus for, the things that would have kept Lazarus with her. However, Jesus knew that Martha needed more than a single healing miracle; Martha needed what all humanity needs: a resurrection God. Jesus did not gloss over Martha's grief, as we perky Christians are apt to do. Jesus did not quote Martha a verse from the Old Testament, expecting her to feel better and move on. Rather, Jesus worked in the soil of her pain, honoring it as the very place where he would have her full attention and be able to open her eyes to a redemption larger than she had known possible.

Calling Martha toward this larger story, this deeper hope, Jesus asked Martha a question. *Do you believe this?* Jesus did not promise to restore Lazarus or begin to explain how Lazarus's death played into a grander divine scheme that would eventually make perfect sense. Jesus did not, in this moment, devote time to consoling his angry, weeping friend. Jesus simply offered himself and asked if she believed. Did she believe that life stood before her in Jesus? Did she believe, as the prophets and the gospel proclaim, that this was indeed God's world and he had not forgotten her? Did she believe that she could trust God with her sorrow and her fear, that his good heart was working for her in ways beyond her wildest expectation?

This is the question Jesus puts to us all. When our heart has gone dry or hope's worn thin, Jesus will not always provide the relief we seek, but he will ask the question that touches the root of things: *Do we believe?* Do we believe that life is available to us in (and only in) Jesus? Do we believe when hopelessness feels far more powerful than our faith? *Do we believe?* It's a dangerous, risky question, inviting us to a dangerous, risky faith.

Any hope Jesus offered Martha that was not fundamentally fixed in a radical abandonment to God would be short-lived. Even if, four days earlier, Lazarus had been healed, death would call again. Pain and sorrow is constant, but Jesus longed for Martha to see more than her pain and more than her fear. Jesus intended to help Martha see God. When Resurrection and Life stands before you, death is a mere footnote.

Jesus was not winging it, ingeniously making the most of a bad situation. From the very beginning, Jesus intended to stage a crisis where there was nothing to hope in but God. Between the time Martha and Mary asked for Jesus' help and when Jesus actually arrived, the situation had grown worse, not better. Jesus had forced death's hand and would use the occasion to gather everyone's full attention. Jesus had something he intended to say. *God* was the word he desired to speak. But Martha, like each of us, had to decide if she would trust what she had yet to see or understand, if she would believe.

Recently I was praying for Wyatt at bedtime, praying that he would follow Jesus. When I finished, I asked Wyatt if following Jesus was something he wanted to do. "Yes," he said, "but I don't know where he's going." I believe Martha would understand Wyatt's dilemma.

Jesus' question touches the rawest nerve of my issues with God. When I wonder if God is real and if following him is foolish, I often resort to making demands. Prove yourself, I say. Give me one, just one, unmistakable sign that you are who you say you are, I order. Most often, silence answers.

A couple years ago, we were driving back from Little Rock, Arkansas, where my fifty-something mother-in-law, Cherry, married a charming fifty-something man named Loren, compliments of eHarmony.com. Dr. Neil Clark Warren must be quite the matchmaker because Cherry had an engagement ring on her finger within three weeks of their first email exchange. We saw the blushing couple off in their limo and then pulled out of Little Rock to head home. After a long drive, we pulled into Tupelo, Mississippi, to spend the night. We had driven through rain showers on and off throughout the day, and a raucous lightning and thunderstorm kicked into gear as we motored into the city. Wyatt, three years old at the time, was enamored with the flashing and the booming. After the sky had been still for a few minutes, he wanted more.

"I want more lightning," he said.

"Well, you'll have to talk to God about that," said his mom.

So, he did. "God," Wyatt said in his cute, scratchy voice, "more lightning." It was an endearing kid moment, the kind when you wish the video were running.

Immediately, my cynicism surfaced in mental dialogue. *Yeah, God*, I pitched skyward. *Give us lightning . . . if you are really there.* It's ludicrous how I approach God as if he were a well-trained circus act or a deified version of Pavlov's dogs. But I often act as though it is God's job, his duty, to convince me he is real, to overcome my doubts.

Jesus, however, stands undaunted by our distrust and our demands. God does not wring his hands, fretful to prove himself or to pile up assurances to barter for our faith. God simply stands there, offering nothing but himself, and asks us the plainest question, *Do you believe?*

Paul Tournier suggests that belief, rather than being something one comes by easily, is something one holds to in spite of whatever evidence we have to the contrary. Jesus has never offered a quaint and docile faith. He offers a gritty, messy faith, a faith that pushes us to our limits and asks us for absolutely everything.

Up to this point, Mary had been conspicuously absent in the narrative. Mary is a beautiful soul in the Jesus-story, all heart, passion run wild. Sometime before, the disciples scolded her for wasting her expensive perfume when, extravagantly, she washed Jesus' feet with it, letting a year's wages run down between Jesus' toes. Mary had always wanted to be near Jesus, effusive in her devotion, full of anticipation. Not now. When Jesus arrived in Bethany and Martha went to meet him and speak her piece, Mary sat alone in her dark room, grieving.

Jesus refused to leave Mary to her isolated space, however, and he requested she come to him. Overcome with disappointment and anger, as Mary neared Jesus, her tears and disillusioned words spilled out: "If you had just been here, Jesus, none of this . . . How could you?" The one who had loved the most had been wounded the deepest, and now Mary collapsed at Jesus' feet, a heartbroken sister.

What emotion would I expect Jesus to experience in response to his suffering friend? Would Jesus sense regret that he handled this exigent crisis so poorly? Would he feel uneasy, fumbling and stuttering, uncertain of how to deal with a psychologically volatile woman? Scripture says Jesus grew angry.

Angry?

We can easily miss the force of Jesus' inflamed reaction. Modern translations have chosen to tone down this seemingly inappropriate response. A common reading offers a Jesus who was "deeply moved in spirit and troubled" (NIV) or (even blander) "terribly upset" (CEV). Translators of older versions, similarly confused by Jesus' unseemly emotion, worked hard to smooth the rough edges and mellow the description of Jesus' outrage. Other translators offer a disheartened Jesus who "sighed" (NEB) in discontent or who "groaned" (ASV) out of weary disenchantment. However, the word John uses to depict Jesus' internal disposition is *embrimaomai*, a coarse, earthy word. *Embrimaomai* describes a visceral reaction of anger, one that fits well with a barroom brawl or a moment when tempers erupt. Jesus was angry, plain and simple.

Jesus was not venting on a distraught Mary or exhibiting a fly-off-the-handle anger. This was anger blended with tears. "Jesus wept," John tells us. There is a vital distinction between being angry *at* someone and being angry *for* someone. The devastation of this fallen, sick world is a tragedy worthy of angry tears, worthy of God's tears. All of this horror should never have been. Here Jesus stood, knee-deep in his creature's havoc, and rage rose in his bones as he faced, firsthand, the suffering and devastation of the human condition. Jesus was immersed in the wreckage of a world he had once called good. Death's stench engulfed him. Evil and desolation ignited his fury. Jesus was mad *for* Mary, but Jesus was mad *at* hell. We were not created for such suffering. Believing was never supposed to be so difficult.

For some, anger immobilizes, turning them passive or timorous. Not Jesus. He stepped in front of the gathered crowd and demanded the stone door of the tomb be removed. Martha, always the practical one, protested. It had been four days, and the decomposing flesh would reek. Who needed another reminder of how foul death is? Curiously, John added here a seemingly unnecessary description: "Martha, the sister of the dead man . . ." (v. 39). John wanted to make absolutely certain we remembered how far gone this situation was. In case somehow amid the dialogue and the action, we had forgotten, this was a *dead* man. A rotting, stinking corpse lay in this tomb.

Still, Jesus insisted. "Move the stone," he said. And when they obeyed, Jesus said in words bold and loud, "Lazarus, come out!"

Lazarus stepped out of the tomb.

Scripture doesn't record what Lazarus uttered as he miraculously emerged, but the presence of this former cadaver echoed loud and clear the word *God*. This is the word more vital than comfort, more urgent than relief, the only word big enough to rouse faith when our will and our heart suggest we have none.

I imagine the crowd seeing Lazarus and spontaneously erupting with hysteric joy. Then, just as quickly, I imagine the moment turning eerily silent as the awe of the miracle settled in. I imagine Jesus turning, scanning all the mystified and euphoric faces, catching the eye of one here and one there. Next I imagine his deliberate look at Martha, at Mary, at Lazarus. Then, in a voice loud enough for all to hear: "Now—do you believe?"

9

Why Do You Doubt?

Faith's Odd Friend

Whether your faith is that there is a God or that there is not a God, if you don't have any doubts, you are either kidding yourself or asleep.

Frederick Buechner

I remember when, for the first extended season (probably a year or more), I couldn't shake the intruding fear that God might really not exist, that my prayers really were as empty and futile as they felt. This gloomy space was incredibly inconvenient—I was a pastor. I had experienced similar, though more fleeting, feelings years earlier in my college library, cuddling one of Karl Barth's biblical treatises. I mean, if you can't have confidence in God when you are a pastor and while you are surrounded by centuries of the church's best thinkers, what does that say about your faith?

Perhaps my weak-kneed devotion explains my affinity for the apostle Peter, the guy who had great spiritual passion and the best of intentions but who, on more than one occasion (and when everybody was watching), just couldn't muster faith. Peter should be my patron saint.

One of Peter's unflattering moments took place one stormy night as Jesus' disciples were tossed about by a furious gale on the Sea of Galilee. Whitecapped waves crashed over the stern and relentlessly battered the wooden vessel from every side, almost snapping the boat in two. To make matters worse, after the besieged shipmen had gone toe-to-toe with the storm nearly all night, they saw an apparition hovering over the raucous waters and heading their direction. Some nights will just never end.

As the figure drew closer, they heard a familiar voice. This was no ghost out in the storm, on top of the sea. This was Jesus. "Don't be afraid," he said. Peter answered with an improbable suggestion. "Lord, if it's you . . . tell me to come to you on the water." Peter exhibited quick, bold faith. If I were in a tempest, surrounded by roaring wind and crashing waves and confronted by an unidentified supernatural phenomenon, a request for an invitation into the black ocean would not be my first reaction.

Jesus answered simply, "Come."

And Peter did. He stepped right out of the boat and into (*onto*, actually) the whipping, swirling water. He walked on the waves. We don't know how far Peter got. One step or twenty, it doesn't really matter. When you walk on water, who's counting? Soon, though, Peter was distracted. Who wouldn't be with the rumbling wind and the madcap waves smashing all about? Peter looked away from Jesus, allowed the storm to capture his attention and began to sink. Going under, Peter managed only a few words. "Lord, save me!"

"Immediately" (what a beautiful word!) Jesus reached down into the frenzied waves, grabbed Peter, and pulled him out of danger. Holding his shivering friend, Jesus asked, "You of little faith, . . . why did you doubt?"

These words have launched a thousand sermons. Most of them volley rapid-fire injunctions: *Don't doubt. Never question God. Have faith—never act uncertain (if you do, you just might drown).* These sermons do not linger with the story. They do not slow down to feel the wind or the fear or to hear Jesus' tone. Eager to rush to an action point, they dumb Scripture's textured narrative down to an easily distilled moralism, a mandate, something we are to do. "We live today in a world impoverished of story," says Peterson, "so it is not surprising that many of us have picked up the bad habit of extracting 'truths' from the stories we read. . . ." When read this unfortunate way, the story of the storm and Peter's hesitation serves primarily to level an indictment against any faith that stumbles or hesitates.

However, what if the story actually *is* the point? What if "the way the Bible is written (narrative) is every bit as important as what is written in it?" Biblical narrative offers a panoramic vision of God active in his world. It reveals to us the reality of what it is to be human, living in relationship with (and often in conflict with) our God. Biblical story gives space for the full human experience, space for the process of faith, for the questions, for the learning and the failures, and for the glorious hope that comes on those occasions when we have walked the journey and arrived (finally) in a place of humble obedience and faith.

Much Christian proclamation lives in the world of pretend, in the theoretical world of "should." We shouldn't doubt. We shouldn't feel rage. We shouldn't crave sex with our office mate. Fine. Maybe. But we do. What then? "Shoulds" and "don'ts" work hard to keep our world sterile. When we confront faithlessness and selfishness and gluttony and addictions, we can safely hide behind the simple assertion of what we should and should not do. No need to deal with anything deeper. No need to wrestle with what dark force or sad lie has laid claim to our heart. Keep it safe and simple and clean. Should. Don't.

If I desire to live honestly *and* if "shoulds" are all Scripture has to offer me, then I truly am alone. Thankfully, Scripture rolls up its sleeves and gets dirty. Scripture does not live in the world as it ought to be, but in the world as it actually is. Jesus does not repeatedly nag me about the kind of faith I should have, but he engages me in the struggle, where I am, right in the middle of my mess.

This is where we find Jesus, in the middle of Peter's mess, but we see Jesus there only if we are immersed in the story and refuse to rush past the details. Jesus did not tell Peter, "Don't doubt." Rather, Jesus did something quite different. He asked Peter *why?* Had Jesus chosen to rebuke Peter with a flat moralism or to slap him with an imperative about possessing faith that is either all in or all out, the conversation would have been over. Peter would have felt shame or regret or anger. Peter would not, however, have been invited to explore further what was happening in his soul that kept him from freely trusting Jesus. Jesus didn't harangue Peter about his failure. Jesus didn't offer a sermon on the virtues of faith and the evils of doubt. Rather, Jesus exhibited one of the sure signals of friendship: curiosity. Jesus entered into Peter's experience and used this geography—doubt and fear and faith worn thin—to get to deeper things. If Jesus had been most concerned with proper behavior, he would have simply plopped Peter back on the deck and said, "Now, don't ever do that again."

Unfortunately, the church has often abandoned Jesus' way of asking questions. We are often most concerned about behavior, about people having the right answers and showing up at the right times—people just doing what they're supposed to do, for crying out loud. We like our messes tidied up quickly. We like our spirituality to be like Quikrete, the small-batch concrete mix that dries in mere minutes. No waiting. No process. No ambiguity. Just the fix. Now.

Not long ago, I chatted with a friend who finds himself pretty angry these days. I asked him how he felt about God. He paused before responding, "I want God to leave me alone."

We have two choices in a moment like this. We can panic at the very thought that someone would say such a thing and whip out our quick responses about how God is good and how obedience is always best. If we do, our message is plain: *There are some things you are simply not allowed to feel. Stop feeling them.* The other, wiser choice would be open curiosity, to wonder—with them—about where in their story these feelings emanate, what kind of God they are imagining when they hope for distance, what they are afraid of, where they have been disappointed.

The first choice works out of fear and abruptly stifles the conversation, the pilgrimage into deeper truths. The second choice trusts God, knows that fear and doubt are not the final

Holy Curiosity

story, and plunges in to discover what God is busy redeeming in our wounded heart.

Rather than sprinting to a standard-issue condemnation against doubt, Scripture encourages us to allow the story to guide us into engaging Jesus' question. Why do *we* doubt? Where does our hesitation come from? It's interesting that Matthew does not record any answer from Peter. By leaving us to wonder what response Peter might have given, we are provided plenty of space to poke around the question for ourselves. For me, a quick answer emerges. I often doubt because, over the years, I've been fed a lot of bull, and some of it came with God's name attached. I don't want to be duped again.

When I was growing up, I remember hearing several preachers say that anytime I felt guilt about something (anything), I best pay attention—God was sending me a harsh message that I had engaged in evil and had better stop it. When I was a little older, I attended a Bible college that worked hard to convince us that Billy Graham was just a shade shy of the Antichrist. Early influences in my life suggested that Dr. Martin Luther King Jr. was a charlatan to be reviled, a Communist stooge. Recently I received a personal email from the widow of the former prime minister of Kurdisdekistan informing me that her husband had tragically died from a heart ailment, and (for tax reasons I couldn't quite follow) she wanted to wire me 14.3 million dollars as soon as I provided her my bank information and social security number. I doubted each of these assertions.

I've doubted political ads and telemarketers offering free cruises and theological fearmongering and empty come-ons from a lonely heart or two. We have lots of promises flung around, lots of loud voices insisting they are selling the truth. Mostly, all lies. A certain level of skepticism does us good in our world. We need some vigilance to keep from being snookered. George MacDonald believed that healthy doubt demonstrated our desire to live honestly: "Thou doubtest because thou lovest the truth."

One afternoon Wyatt sat in the living room entranced by a TV commercial. When it concluded, he had a burning question. "Are my tennis shoes Skechers?" he asked. To his disappointment, I told him they weren't. Without hesitation, Wyatt passionately insisted his next pair must be because he had just learned a bit of critical information. "On the commercial," Wyatt insisted, "they said that Skechers has the coolest styles." We all learn that not everything we read or hear, not everything spoken with authority, is actually true.

Questioning provides a vital tool for a maturing faith. Our questions slow us from jumping naively after every sound bite or after every huckster pimping his snake oil. Doubt is a normal part of learning and growing and working your way between what is real and what is not, what is true and what is false. Doubt is inextricably linked to the process of learning whom we can trust. I have found doubt to be a surprisingly good friend when used evenly, as an equal opportunity offender. I once heard Philip Yancey say we ought to doubt our doubts as much as we doubt our faith. That sounds about right to me, evidenced by the verbiage on one of my T-shirts: "I have my doubts about disbelief."

The early catechisms took shape as a series of questions, exploring truth via the route of questioning, being open to the myriad possibilities. Our convictions of truth might end up as dogma, but they begin as questions. Karl Barth said, "In this sense, doubt simply marks the fact that nothing in theology is self-evident. Nothing can be had for nothing. Everything must be worked through in order to acquire validity." Honest questions signal that we take God and his truth seriously, serious enough to work it over to see whether it stands up or crumples under scrutiny.

Questions are also vital for faith because they indicate that we are honest and engaged in the process. I'm concerned when Christians never have questions and are never troubled by the dissonance between the peace, justice, and hope God promises and the violence, injustice, and despair thriving so vibrantly in our world. If faith is, as the Hebrews writer suggests, having eyes to see what we actually cannot see—if our difficulty is, as Paul says, squinting through the foggy, dim light—then we ought to have some questions, some places of profound wrestling. When we are perplexed about these disparities and the implications for God's reliability, we evidence how we give God's claims their just weight—and how we expect him to come through on his promises.

Another reason we doubt is simply this: we're human. We ought not to despise our proclivity to doubt—it is part of being made from dust, part of being finite in conversation with the Infinite. There is much we don't know, much we can't see clearly. Honesty demands we reckon with this truth. As G. K. Chesterton liked to say, it is only materialists or madmen who have never doubted. For many of us, doubt is simply part of our Christian experience. We can rail against it and malign it and shame people for it all we want—the truth remains that doubt holds a place in our story. Most of God's saints wrangled with doubt. Martin Luther, Charles Spurgeon, St. John of the Cross, Mother Teresa (who said, "If I ever become a Saint—I will surely be one of 'darkness'"), Mary, David, Job, Noah, Moses— each of them were familiar with the soul's dark, questioning terrain.

Most of us desire sturdy faith. We want to believe in God and have it stick, but belief slips free (in part) because we are frail beings with limitations and short sight and the inability (at times) to comprehend what God could possibly be up to. "We turn toward love like sunflowers to the sun," said Anne Lamott, "and then the human parts kick in. This seems to me the only real problem, the human parts—the body, for instance, and the mind."

When Jesus encountered doubters, he did not leave them to wallow in their uncertainty, but neither did he rail against their human frailty. Jesus showed his pierced hands to Thomas. Jesus met with Nicodemus in the middle of the night. Jesus healed the demon-possessed son of the father who pleaded, "I do believe; help me overcome my unbelief!" And here, with Peter, Jesus did not leave him to drown, nor did he heap vitriol on his wavering faith. Rather, Jesus pulled Peter from the water and asked him a question. *Why?*

Doubt takes root in us for yet another reason. We are committed to self-protection. We have been wounded too often, fed lies too many times; and now, we are slow to trust, slow to believe, slow to allow ourselves to live open and free, childlike. We wear heavy steel armor around our heart, virtually every inch pitted and dented by all the half-truths and broken promises and manipulative words that have been lobbed in our direction. The shield came in handy; it deflected numerous blows. But now, the cold steel suffocates our soul. It blocks the warm, free sun from our heart. Our safety will soon kill us, if it hasn't already. To live, we must throw our armor aside.

It is one thing to doubt because we are committed to the truth and are unsure whether we have found it. There's even some nobility there. However, to doubt because we are afraid of the truth, afraid of what it might ask of us or afraid of the risk inherently attached whenever we say, without hesitation, "This I believe . . ."—to doubt simply because we are afraid of living otherwise holds no nobility at all. Alfred Korzybski said, "There are two ways to slide easily through life: Namely, to believe everything or to doubt everything; both ways save us from thinking." And, I would add, both ways save us from the risk of trusting.

Doubt as a barrier to trust is where Jesus takes aim. Jesus doesn't mind questions. He gives time and space for people to hear and consider and journey into the truth. Peter's doubt, in fact, had nothing to do with philosophical quandaries or historical veracity. Peter did not have a theological dilemma.

Peter did not slip into the waves because of an existential crisis. Peter wavered in trusting his friend. His issue was not creedal; it was relational.

Whatever pushed Peter to doubt, it was obviously connected to fear, understandably so. The disciples had been on pins and needles the entire night. In a quick turn of events, Peter found himself alone on top of the waves out in the middle of a blustery storm. This doubt had nothing to do with logic or reason. There was no process that led Peter here. An apologetics lecture or a philosophical conversation would not have helped. Often we believe our doubt would be assuaged if God would miraculously intervene in our world. No miracles would have aided Peter. He had just lived the miracle, a few extraordinary aquatic steps. Peter's doubt detonated, in a flash, because all of a sudden he thought he might drown—and his fear was larger than his trust in Jesus.

Jesus did not ask Peter why he had a mental dilemma or why he lacked dogmatic certainty on the Torah's teaching. Jesus asked Peter why, after all he had experienced, he did not trust in Jesus' friendship and in his ability to protect him. Why did Peter choose to look away? Why did he freeze and stop moving toward Jesus? I know this place well. My doubt has maxed out its usefulness when, rather than keeping me honest, humble, and in search of truth, it keeps me immobilized, refusing to trust or to engage God. Matthew's story does not deride doubts that keep us moving and questioning, but it cautions strongly against any doubt that stops us in our tracks or that suffocates our inquisitive imagination of what God might be working. Author Frank Rees said, "To have faith, in Matthew's sense, is to be open to the surprising possibilities of God and of ourselves."

Doubt's dastardly side turns us into cynics, into narrow, unimaginative people afraid to believe in anything beyond our control, unwilling to commit to much of anything more obvious than the existence of our own nose. Joe Bayly lamented the hardship faith discovers when it runs up against entrenched doubt. "If I were a twin in the womb I doubt that I could prove the existence of earth to my mate. He would probably object that the idea of an earth beyond the womb was ridiculous, that the womb was the only earth we'd ever know."

Doubt is our enemy—not when it makes us unsure of certain facts, but when it holds us back from trusting in the person of Jesus, when it folds us into cynicism and causes us to live in the smallness of eternal hesitation. As Alister McGrath said, "Faith and doubt aren't mutually exclusive—but faith and unbelief are." Doubt, at its best, opens me up to consider intently all I am experiencing, prodding me to hope for and move toward truth. Doubt, at its worst, closes me off to all I am experiencing, snuffing out hope altogether.

This is why doubt, if it becomes our identity or a reality unto itself, will always make us more guarded, more fearful, less curious. This ravaging doubt stunts our best, brightest, most expansive human qualities, making us less playful, less creative, less courageous, less eager, and far less generous. Doubt might serve well as one of the voices on our path to truth, but when doubt becomes the judge and jury, the final interpreter of the story, it crushes our soul. It smothers trust. It closes our heart to God.

Every relationship requires an open heart, leaning toward the other with hope. I must not wait to see how my sons will respond to my fatherly love before I give it. I must not wait to see if my wife will return my affection before I reach out to kiss her. Faith, love, friendship—each demand risk. We must decide to love. We must walk with determination toward friendship. We must, at some point, abandon ourselves to the God whose kindness and goodness have won our trust, even though chaos swells all around us.

I have a friend who gets lost in her mind's winding, gloomy labyrinth. As soon as a ray of hope pierces, a thousand questions and "what ifs" push it back out. We have good conversations because I see myself in her. I know what it is to never allow yourself to stand on solid ground, to never rest that you have heard the truth, to never truly receive from someone because you are always on guard, hypervigilant. It's miserable and lonely and a tiny, tiny space. We cannot live that way if we want to be whole, alive. At some point, if we want to live, we will have to trust, to surrender to the God who invites us to "Come." We will have to take a step, and when we fall or grow fearful or are disappointed, we will have to decide—again—whether we choose life, whether we will trust for yet another dangerous step.

Søren Kierkegaard said that to have faith, we must "venture a decisive act. The proof does not precede but follows; it exists in and with the life that follows Christ." We really cannot know for sure whether God will rescue us until God actually has opportunity for rescue, until we fling our arms out and fall forward, leaving nothing but wind and God to catch us.

10

What Do You Want?

A Way Back to God

Hope always draws the soul from the beauty which is seen to what is beyond, always kindles the desire for the hidden from what is constantly perceived.

Gregory of Nyssa

"Well," said Pooh, "what I like best"—and then he had to stop and think. Because although Eating Honey was a very good thing to do, there was a moment just before you began to eat it which was better than when you were, but he didn't know what it was called.

A. A. Milne

Someone once asked Jesus which was the greatest of all the commandments. Provided similar opportunity, I would ask Jesus which was the greatest of all his questions. I imagine he would answer with some version of the question he posed in two different moments (with vastly different outcomes): *what do you want?* Does any question cut quicker to what is real and true in us? Does any question leave us more exposed? Is any question harder to answer truthfully?

In Eden, enfleshed in a piece of forbidden fruit, a stark choice sat before Adam and Eve: do you want self-knowledge or do you want God? *What do you most want?* The Mosaic covenant embodied the choice Israel would have to make, the choice between death and life. *Which did they want?* And for us: the wide path or the narrow path, self or joy, God or relief? *What do we want?*

This word—*want*—can be translucent, a word we stare right through without noticing. I want another helping of mac-n-cheese. I want the crabgrass in my yard to surrender. My preschool sons want a bike and a bug kit and to be a super-hero and the world to stop being at war and a Pop-Tart. We want a lot of things; but when you stack them all together, it doesn't feel like we really want anything at all.

From God's mouth, however, *want* is a solid word, a mass of earth and granite standing in our path. God is eager to hear what our heart craves, what will cause us to go mad if we do not have it. God wonders what has captured our hope and our imagination and our energy. God wonders if, with all our wanting, we want him.

One biblical encounter Mark relates places this holy curiosity in the fore. Jesus and the disciples were on their way to Jerusalem when they passed a blind beggar on the road who hoped for a few coins to be tossed his way. The beggar couldn't see the commotion moving toward him, but he heard the noise of feet and voices and felt the swelling energy from the gathering crowd. He heard someone mention the prophet's name, Jesus of Nazareth, and something in the blind beggar quickened, prompting him to shout, "Jesus, Son of David, have mercy on me!" The title the beggar attached to Jesus, "son of David," was a messianic title, rich in history and anticipation. From childhood, the beggar had heard of one who would come and salvage Israel, bringing healing and restoration, making all things right.

And here Jesus stood. Hope and potent desire ruptured in this man, rendering an ironic miracle, a precursor to the healing that would follow. This blind man was able to see what even the disciples had yet to see, and he shouted it: Jesus was the Son of David. With this vision, the blind man could not compose himself. The beggar couldn't hold it in. He had to get Jesus' attention. He *had* to.

The crowd near the beggar told him to hush; it is annoying when those who are supposed to stay quiet don't. The shouting beggar was undeterred. When we are powerless and desperate yet still clinging to life, we refuse to be silenced. In fact, Mark says the blind man, in response to the crowd's scowling attempts to muffle him, ratcheted up his appeals. He "shouted all the more." And it worked. Jesus heard the beggar's shouts, and Jesus asked the man to come to him. Even though Jesus was traveling into the crucible of his final week, he paused to help a poor, blind man. The beggar on the edge of the road was no detour.

And then came that all-important question. W*hat do you want?*

What impresses me most in Mark's story is the man's immediate, unpretentious reply. "Rabbi, I want to see." He didn't want coins or fish. He was blind, and he didn't want to be blind any longer. Jesus responded just as quickly: "Go, your faith has healed you."

Uncovering our deepest desires is onerous work. Smothered, forgotten, or shamed into hiding, our true desires often lie fallow. They are buried under years of disappointment, disconnection, fear, and outright manipulation. Our culture, addicted to shallow or nihilistic passions detached from God, provides little help. We need a wise, fierce friend to probe past the facade and quarry into our hidden places. We need a strong hand to grab hold of our entombed, comatose heart, wake it up, and lead it back to God. We need Jesus.

Rarely do we encounter the kind of friendship Jesus pursued with the beggar. If we hope to truly know someone, we must uncover what the person's heart longs for, and this uncovering takes time, space, questions. As theologian Frederick Bruner put it, Jesus was in a "search for a conversation." Jesus knew the question that wedges into the axis of who we are: *what do you want?* Yet in our normal experience, we seldom hear this question. When was the last time we were curious enough about the texture of another's soul to wonder what he or she wants, hopes for, or what presses the person to tears or incites laughter? When was the last time another was curious enough about us, not what we do or what we know or what we can offer—but *us*, to ask us what we desire in our life? Nobody asks the simplest question. Most of our experience works to kill desire, not spur it on.

Both my sons, Wyatt and Seth, live with desire turned full throttle. Wyatt is five, and his questions are infinite. He has an innocent, animated ambition to discover and learn. Recently he figured out how to use a screwdriver, and while any hardware secured by screws is no longer safe in our house, the boyish pleasure he finds in tearing things apart delights me. Wyatt believes the entire world holds wonder, and he wants to see it. Seth is four and is the life of the party, the kid who has never met a stranger. He greets people with a gregarious, playful smile that says, "C'mon, how could you not love this?" If Seth's personality were a shirt, it would be tie-dye all the way.

I love how both of them are open to the world, open with desire. I will rue the day when someone tells Wyatt to stop getting so excited about discovery, that his inquisitiveness is too much to handle. I will lament whenever Seth hears a sour voice telling him to tone down the enthusiasm, that it's just silly to live so unbridled. I fear for the fate of their uncurbed desire that, for today, hangs out, flying free for everyone to see.

I fear for my sons because I know my own story. I see my places of timidity, how I draw back too often from boyish passions. I see how I have listened to the droning voices urging caution, warning against foolishness or making a mistake. Fearful, guarded, disconnected from desire—that is not what I want. What I *want* is to live with chutzpah, to sing louder than I should, to kiss my wife like a madman, to yank my clunky, off-beat dance out of hiding and take it to the streets, not giving one whit who sees. I want to be the man George Meyer, the creator of *The Simpsons*, describes, who will "chase down his passions, wrestle them to the dirt, and ride them like ostriches." I want to love my boys as only a man flinging himself into the world is able to love. I want to fight for my wife's heart like a man with nothing to withhold. I want to run after my God like a man born anew. I want to risk and hope with reckless disregard for propriety and safety.

In our fallen world, living this authentically, this awake, requires great courage and grit. Prevailing culture and our own fearful hiding are not desire's only enemies. Sadly, the church is often a menace as well.

The church should be desire's guardian. We need the church's prophetic voice to speak the truth loud. We yearn for God's community to counter the messages of our culture and our own self-protective addictions. We long for the church to guide us along the messy path of discovering and nurturing our God-given desires, teaching us how to honor desire more not less. We need guides to instruct us in the simplest spiritual maxim: if we abandon small desires (sin), we are free to crave large desires (God). We need the church to insist, as St. Augustine has, that the "entire life of a good Christian is in fact an exercise of holy desire."

The truth, however, is that Christian communities are often a perilous environment for desire. Long wary of the dangers of passions run amok, the church has often opted simply to kill desire altogether and be done with it. We do violence to desire by unloading flat moralisms, leveraging fear-heavy guilt, and ferociously quashing anyone too alive, too hazardous, too out-of-bounds. This suffocating perspective follows a distorted creedal mantra for the Christian heart: better dead and limp than alive and dangerous.

For instance, *accountability* is a Christian buzzword. Designed to aid spiritual formation, the (good) intention is to walk and struggle and live honestly with a spiritual friend who knows our foibles and our mess and loves us toward Jesus anyway. However, accountability often devolves into a spiritual lashing, when we attempt to manage our behavior by the sheer terror of having to 'fess up. Numerous lists of questions have been designed to serve the accountability process, but they usually tread shallow water, only uncovering external scandalous behaviors: Have I looked at porn this week? Have I used my money wisely? Have I given emotional intimacy to someone other than my husband? However, I have never—not once—seen Jesus' question make the list: *what do I want?*

This is not to say all desire is good. Much of our desire is malign. Twisted desire is desire separated from God and God's intentions. Twisted desire is the underbrush that must be cleared to allow room for true desire to grow. Mark provides a stark contrast to the story of the blind beggar, highlighting how Jesus intends to probe past puny, distorted desires to unearth true desires.

Earlier in the narrative, two brothers, Jesus' disciples James and John, approached Jesus with a brash request. "We want you to do for us whatever we ask," they said. Their crass appeal might seem less bald-faced if we knew that the words emerged out of the previous conversation when Jesus announced that the disciples would find reward in his kingdom that was to come. The brothers liked the idea of reward and apparently were in the mood to haggle remunerative details. Still, when we see the blunt proposition—"do whatever we ask"—here in plain black and white, it appears so brazen. Yet Jesus didn't flinch. "What do you want me to do for you?" he asked.

If there was any ambiguity about John and James's impertinence, it evaporated with their presumptive reply. "Arrange it . . . so that we will be awarded the highest places of honor in your glory—one of us at your right, the other at your left." I'm curious when James or John awoke the next morning, with a bit clearer head, did one of them wonder, *Did I really say that?*

Jesus' reply cut them short: "You have no idea what you are asking." To follow Jesus so intimately, they would have to face suffering they would be unable to endure. They would be unable to "drink the cup" Jesus would soon drink. Further, James and John's desires were trite, small. Jesus' issue with James and John was not that they asked for too much. Jesus was not put off by their boldness, as if desire itself were the vice he intended to scrub clean. Jesus rebuked the brothers because their desire was a false desire. It was too small. Jesus offered them God in the flesh, the scandalous mercy of a kingdom come—and James and John were jockeying for seating arrangements. They did not know what they truly wanted.

When I have conversations with couples preparing for marriage, one of the areas I believe crucial to help them explore is their desire. Recently I sat with an engaged couple and asked them why they chose each other. The guy fumbled with a few lines about how they complemented one another well. One was messy; one was not. One would be discouraged; the other would have high spirits. It all sounded very sensible, but the problem was they easily could have said the same sorts of things about their mechanic or a pet ferret. The woman also supplied a tidy laundry list of reasons to say "I do," but I knew there were intense desires she had not awakened. What was missing from the answer—what I really wanted to hear—was crazy passion. I wanted eyes to light up and palms to go sweaty. I wanted them to say moony things about the other's gorgeous smile and cute toes, to hear how they could hardly keep their hands off one another. I would have welcomed a giggle or two. I knew there was more. Despite their dispassionate lists, I knew they had desires much deeper than the drivel offered. They were both creative and passionate—and in love. However, they needed help connecting to their rich heart. I cannot tell them what they want. They have to speak it for themselves. So I ended our time together asking them to consider two questions: what in the other brings you pleasure and delight? and what do you want from the other person? Our deep longings are always with us, but sometimes we need help pulling them to the surface.

Jesus loves to pull our desires to the surface, and he loves when our desires (especially our truest, deepest ones) come into the open freely. Jesus loved the blind man's request because it was honest and raw. Jesus loved how the blind man was quick with his hope; he loved his fiery desire. Jesus didn't quibble. The only thing Jesus cared to do was give the man what he wanted.

Both Jesus and Mark took great pleasure in this man who flung his desire into the open. Mark hinted there was something uncommon about this beggar when he introduced him by his name: Bartimaeus. The introduction is significant because nowhere else does Mark provide the name of a person Jesus healed. The blind man's tenacious passion was so uninhibited and bare that he simply could not go unnoticed, unnamed. Even more intriguing, Mark made certain we heard that Bartimaeus was the "son of Timaeus," literally meaning "son of honor." This blind beggar, even when pushed to the fringes, clung to his untamed hopes; and in time he (ironically) received exactly what the misguided disciples had angled for—honor.

Haven't we enjoyed the pleasure of experiencing a woman or man who is dissatisfied with trivial whims and who pushes right into their true desires? Any man who, like Bartimaeus, moves solidly into his desire and his world, refusing to hide his true self, is a man we admire. Any woman who refuses to chill her heart or veil her beauty or tame her voice or wilt under the heat of expectations and convention—this is a woman in whom we all delight. When we catch a glimpse of her, we drink her in, even as we attempt to regain our breath. Poet Tony Hoagland describes the wonder of such an encounter: "[W]hen she walks into the room/ . . . we take our . . . hands/out of our pockets, and clap."

How then do we learn to know our true desires, particularly when so much resists us taking that path? How did Bartimaeus instinctively know what he wanted while James and John didn't have the first idea? Why is it that so often when someone is curious to know what we want, to put words to the deepest longings of our soul, we have no idea how to begin? We stammer and stumble or mumble a lame answer we know is really no answer at all. Like James and John, we don't know what we are asking.

One of Miska's favorite questions to ask in the little spiritual community that gathers in our home is one she borrowed from the old spiritual guides: *what dwells in your soul?* Often, when people first hear her question, it evokes unease. People don't know where to go with it. Mark Twain said his difficulty was not helping a person get what they wanted. That was easy. Twain's difficulty was finding a person who knew what they wanted in the first place. We struggle to answer the question of what we want because we simply do not know.

We also struggle because we get hung up in our attempts to constantly evaluate whether or not our desire is appropriate. We don't know if it is okay to say, "I want a great sex life" or "I'd really like a new Lamborghini." In our effort to continually monitor if we are feeling whatever we believe we are supposed to feel, we short-circuit our ability to be in tune with whatever we actually *do* feel, acceptable or not. Sometimes propriety needs to take a backseat to honesty. A first step to moving toward passionate desire for God is to be able to be aware of—and own—all the smaller desires distracting our heart.

In contrast, Bartimaeus knew what he wanted because he had paid attention to his pain. For years he had seen only darkness. Bartimaeus had been blind so long he didn't know his own figure; the years had formed him into a man he had never seen. But he had not lost himself amid all the years. Bartimaeus had not shut down; he remembered. And now, on this day, pain proved his friend. When Jesus asked Bartimaeus what he wanted, his anguish hurled out an answer: "I want to see!"

Frederick Buechner says that tears are essential guides. "Whenever you find tears in your eyes, . . ." he says, "it is well to pay the closest attention. They are not only telling you something about the secret of who you are, but more often than not God is speaking to you through them of the mystery of where you have come from and is summoning you to where, if your soul is to be saved, you should go next." Recently I was talking to Miska about a bedtime interaction I saw between her and one of our sons. As I began to tell her the grace I saw in her tenderness, tears took me by surprise. Usually I succumb to the temptation to back the tears down, but here, I knew I had to pay attention to where my soul was trying to break free. Tears provide an invaluable gift, a trail to mercy. If we trace our tears, following their salty path up our heart's abandoned ravines, we will find pain pumping wet reminders of what we truly long for, what we most crave.

I met Perry in Boulder, Colorado, because he was hungry. Perry was soiled and foul, a homeless vet who wore his years less gracefully than most. He stumbled up to our street-side table at Noodles and Company, obviously drunk. He asked for our scraps when we were done, wanting whatever pasta he could scavenge. My friend Ken and I invited him to pull up a chair, and I ordered him a meal. Over the next hour, while Perry gobbled his fettuccini and grilled chicken, we encountered a man who had forgotten who he was, a man on the verge of fatally losing touch with what he wanted.

Decades of alcohol and ghastly Vietnam memories had tinkered with Perry's sense of reality. He kept exclaiming, with expletives, that Nixon and Kissinger were heroes. Perry recounted graphic stories of war and a particularly violent memory of seeing a buddy riddled by enemy fire. However, with scratchy voice and reddening, moist eyes, Perry told us his heaviest fear: he would die and never see his grandchildren in New Jersey. He wished he could hold his grandkids in his lap, to love them and be loved in return; but Perry said it was too late for him. This fear, this desire for family, pierced him, but he quickly changed the subject, back to Nam and Nixon.

As our conversation finished, Ken grabbed Perry's gaze and spoke plainly, man to man. "Call your son, Perry. Go home."

I don't know where Perry is today, or even if he is still breathing. Perry didn't belong in a town not his own, bumming pasta from strangers. He had forgotten who he was because he had forgotten what he wanted. If he would only listen, really listen, to his desire for his family . . . if he would allow this desire to gnaw at his gut, eventually, Perry would make that call. Perhaps, eventually, Perry just might begin to find himself again.

Though pain and a hunger for healing are most prominent in Bartimaeus's story, they are not the only forces that awaken desire. Nothing chips at an ossified heart like beauty, and nothing slices through our malaise like faith. God has given us numerous guides to lead us to the true desires he has inscribed on our soul. We need only to listen and follow.

Bartimaeus's desire connected to something deeper than mere physical healing. Bartimaeus was desperate for his redemptive God, the "son of David" on whom all hope and history waits. Mark tells us that when Jesus called to Bartimaeus, the beggar threw his cloak to the side, got up, and ran to him. For a blind beggar, a cloak sustained him, keeping him warm during cold nights and dry during long rains. A beggar collected alms in his coat, and the coat provided his one constant comfort. But what is a coat, what is safety and self-protection and a few meager alms when the God of all hope and desire calls your name?

If we follow Jesus' question deep enough, we will uncover our core desire. This desire is particular, uncluttered. What we truly crave is God. More than friendship, more than sex, more than our life clipping along nicely, we are ravenous for God. If we find ourselves connecting to desires bent entirely inward, narcissistically hoarding and demanding, we have not yet dug far enough. Holy desire—true desire—has an umbilical connection to our original identity and the God who formed it. C. S. Lewis called this holy desire the "signature on each soul." True desire is a mark, a mystery God implanted in us. To know this desire is to know (and to be hungry for more of) God.

Sadly, however, our desire might seem so far gone we honestly don't know where to begin. We need not be overwhelmed with the vast distance or the uncertain terrain; we need only to take the first step. To begin the journey back to God, we don't have to know what we want—we only need to *want* to know what we want.

Not long ago I attended a conference where Eugene Peterson and his son Eric shared speaking duties. I was struck by their interactions and their obvious joy with one another. Being a father, I asked Eugene how he pursued this relationship with Eric. He answered simply, "You only have to want to."

After Words

Many friends model Jesus' way to me, asking and receiving good questions, hard questions, hopeful questions. Corey and Juli Kalbaugh are life friends who love to drink coffee with Miska and me and laugh and pray and consider what God is up to with all of us—that spot on our little couch will always be theirs. Deb Lawson asks the most penetrating questions. Her intensity runs almost as deep as her grace. Debbie Smith enters our home as a friend, and hours of conversation later, the friendship has grown even stronger. Ken Edwards chats with me every other Wednesday, and good Jesus-type questions are normal fare. Recently George Blake has also given his time to sit with me in the questions. Stephen Baldwin and Raul Cruz—you see me and you help me see Jesus. Thank you for being with me, for questioning with me. I am blessed by each of these friends.

Chad Allen has been one fantastic editor on this project. He's had to ask me some tough questions, perhaps more than he'd like; but whatever value you find in these pages owes its presence to Chad. I was often out of sorts as I worked to bring these words to life, and patiently Chad guided me along. Thank you, Chad. Truly.

Miska's questions probe the furthest. She knows my heart, my soul. And she loves me anyway. She keeps asking me where my heart is, where I am. I hope to spend the rest of my years having those kinds of conversations with her. For many, she is a spiritual guide. I am blessed to call her soul mate. Miska, I love you. Always.

Wyatt and Seth are Jesus' voices too. Their innocence and their honesty work together to pose questions that cannot be ignored—I love that. Their range of questions takes me off guard: "What is God doing? Why are you on your computer? Do people's eyebrows die?" Wyatt and Seth, keep asking. Keep listening. I love you with all my heart.

Continuing the Conversation

Chapter 1 When Jesus Calls Us Out

1. What is your small or fearful place from which God might want to pull you?
2. What can we learn from the way, the manner, of Jesus' friendship and teaching—the way he often asked questions rather than gave instructions or principles or facts?

3. What do you think of the possibility that Jesus posed some of his questions because he was genuinely curious and did not know the answers? How does this possibility affect how you relate to Jesus?
4. Has anyone ever asked you a deeply probing question that you couldn't wiggle free from? What was that experience like?

Chapter 2 Who Condemns You?

1. What kind of shaming, judging, or condemning voices have you heard in your life? Where did they come from? What did they say?
2. Have you ever seen the church use shame as a tool to motivate people toward certain behaviors? What does that look like? How does that feel? How does this practice differ from Jesus' way?
3. The author said that when it comes to heaping on shame, "self can be the worst abuser." Do you heap shame on yourself? How?
4. What are the shameful places in your soul (the bare spots) that you hide?

Chapter 3 Why Are You Afraid?

1. What is your deepest fear?
2. Probe deeper. Is there something deeper behind the fear you named? Where do you think your fear comes from?

3. How does your ability (or inability) to control your life, your circumstances, your future affect your experience of fear?

4. "A fear that is ignored and constantly shoved to the edges is not defeated; it is merely given time to sharpen its fangs." How does this mesh with your experience?

Chapter 4 How Much Bread Do You Have?

1. The author suggests we are too "quick to make peace with our hunger." Are there any longings, hungers, or desires that you have shoved to the side or ignored? Why?

2. What kind of famine do you see in your world? Where do you see it?

3. Respond to Toni Morrison's observation: "How exquisitely human was the wish for permanent happiness, and how thin human imagination became trying to achieve it."

4. What are some physical, sacramental (the intersection of the divine and the physical) ways that Jesus meets you and fills you?

Chapter 5 Are You Being Willfully Stupid?

1. The author defines *stupidity* as the willful refusal to see and hear God. Are there any places where you are willfully ignoring what God is doing or saying?

2. "We are often obsessed with codifying God, insisting what he will *always* do and . . . *never* do." How do you face this temptation?

3. What do you make of poet Rainer Rilke's belief that "the only case of courage required of us [is this]: to be courageous in the face of the strangest, the most whimsical and unexplainable thing that we could encounter"?

4. What new things do you believe God might be doing in you?

Chapter 6 My God, Why Have You Abandoned Me?

1. Describe your emotive response to the fact that in Jesus' prayer, he spoke of God abandoning him? Have you ever felt this emotion? Have you ever prayed this way?

2. The author believes we are often "skittish about Jesus' emotions." What do you make of this? Are you comfortable with Jesus being angry or sad or fearful or disappointed (particularly if any of these emotions are directed at God the Father)?

3. Why would we be tempted to gloss over (or even completely ignore) our pain?

4. Respond to Walter Wink's description of biblical prayer as "impertinent, shameless, indecorous . . . more like haggling in an oriental bazaar than the polite monologues of the churches."

Chapter 7 Are You Confused?

1. Where are some of the places where God has confused you, acting differently than you expected?
2. What is your response to the author's suggestion that God at times actually evokes confusion?
3. Where are some places that you need to stretch your spiritual imagination so you can see God at work? What do you think it would look like for you to begin to open yourself up to a more spiritual imagination?
4. How might your disorientation or confusion push you past dead ends and into new God-inspired places?

Chapter 8 Do You Believe This?

1. Do you remember the first time you experienced God's silence? How did you respond?
2. Where are the places in your story that make you want to ask God, "Why?"
3. Do you believe that asking why is a dangerous and risky question? How is it dangerous and risky?
4. What is your reaction to the notion of God being angry *for* you? What are some of the situations in which God would be angry for you?

Chapter 9 Why Do You Doubt?

1. What are your darkest doubts about God and faith?

2. What do you make of this line: "Scripture does not live in the world as it ought to be, but in the world as it actually is"?
3. How different would our interactions with our doubts be if we engaged them (as Jesus did) with curiosity and exploration rather than with fear and immediate rebuke?
4. Where does George MacDonald's statement take you? "Thou doubtest because thou lovest the truth."

Chapter 10 What Do You Want?

1. What messages have you received from the church about the value (or danger) of your desires?
2. Describe an experience when someone was deeply curious about you—your desires, your hopes, your dreams. What was that experience like?
3. What do you think of the author's conviction that "the church should be desire's guardian"? Or of Augustine's belief that the "entire life of a good Christian is in fact an exercise of holy desire"?
4. When have tears or excitement or spurts of joy signaled to you what your true desires are?

Sources

Chapter 1 When Jesus Calls Us Out

10 *It is a great loss.* Daniel Holman and Lonni Collins Pratt, *The Little Book of Hours: Praying with the Community of Jesus* (Brewster, MA: Paraclete Press, 2003), 134.

20 *. . . hands [were] stuffed.* Ibid.

Chapter 2 Who Condemns You?

24 *[O]f all the means.* E. M. Forster, *Howard's End* (New York: Buccaneer Books, 1984), 316.

24 *. . . woman caught in.* John 8:1–11.

26 *. . . censensus that this is.* Zane Hodges offers the most forceful argument that John 8:1–11 indeed was part of the original text in "The Woman Taken in Adultery (John 8:1–11): The Text," *Bibliotheca Sacra* 136 (1979): 318–72. However, the more common view concludes this was not part of the original text. This perspective (along with arguments in favor of its historical legitimacy) are found in Raymond Brown, *The Gospel according to John*, The Anchor Bible (Garden City, New York: Doubleday, 1966); and Craig Blomberg, *The Historical Reliability of John's Gospel* (Downers Grove, IL:

InterVarsity, 2001). Gerald Borchert goes so far as to say that "[f]or most in the Church, Protestants . . . and Roman Catholics alike, this pericope is regarded as being fully canonical, even though it has been understood by textual scholars for centuries to be out of place" (*The Gospel according to John I–XII*, The Anchor Bible, vol. 29 [Nashville: Broadman and Holman, 1996], 369).

27 . . . *punished.* Leviticus 20:10; Deuteronomy 22:22.

29 . . . *mercy and faithfulness."* Matthew 23:23.

32 . . . *he just painted.* Eric Hedegaard, "Alone in the Dark with Kiefer Sutherland," *Rolling Stone*, April 20, 2006, 50.

33 *That is the.* Of course I am using *condemnation* here in the sense of shaming, debasing personhood, and annihilating the human soul and identity. God will, Scripture indicates, allow us to bear the result of our sinful rebellion if we insist on refusing his rescue (Genesis 3, Romans 3).

33 . . . *to sit on your own lap."* Frederick Buechner, *Wishful Thinking: A Seeker's ABC* (San Francisco: HarperSanFrancisco, 1993), 39.

33 . . . *us, in our "helpless.* From Horatio Spafford's "It Is Well with My Soul."

34 . . . *or symbols or markings.* Brown, *Gospel according to John*, 333.

35 . . . *crowd.* It has also been suggested that Jesus might have been pronouncing judgment on the Pharisees and scribes, symbolically enacting Jeremiah's prophecy: "Those who turn away from [the Lord] will be written in the dust" (Jer. 17:13).

36 . . . *will condemn me?"* Isaiah 50:9.

Chapter 3 Why Are You Afraid?

38 *I abandon You, Lord.* St. Thomas Aquinas, *The Aquinas Prayer Book* (Manchester, NH: Sophia Institute Press, 2000), 49; and Leif Enger, *Peace Like a River* (New York: Grove Press, 2001), 3.

38 . . . *respects no law or.* Yann Martel, *Life of Pi* (New York: Harcourt, 2001), 161.

39 . . . *called it a "furious.* Matthew 8:24.

39 . . . *plied an apocalyptic.* Craig L. Blomberg, *Matthew*, vol. 22 of The New American Commentary (Nashville: Broadman Press, 1992), 148.

41 . . . *unknown limits."* Timothy Stanley, "Deconstructing Fear: A Reading of M. Night Shyamalan," from metaphilm.com, at http://metaphilm.com/philm.php?id=411_0_2_0, posted April 19, 2005.

45 . . . *God to save him.* In one of his letters he wrote to Mary Willis, C. S. Lewis suggests it is precisely this reality—Jesus' own experience of fear in Gethsemane—that tells us there is no shame in the sensation of fear. The question, rather, is what we do with our fear. "Fear is horrid, but there's no reason to be ashamed of it. Our Lord was afraid (dreadfully so)

in Gethsemane." *The Collected Letters of C. S. Lewis: Narnia, Cambridge and Joy 1950–1963*, vol. 3 (New York: HarperCollins, 2007), 590.

45 ... *through weakness and testing.* Hebrews 4:15 Message.

45 ... *taught as one who.* Matthew 7:28–29.

46 ... *winds and the waves obey.* Matthew 8:27.

48 ... *on these.* Matthew 8:18–22.

50 ... *your heart take courage.* Psalm 31:24 ESV.

51 ... *not to be feared."* Aquinas, *Aquinas Prayer Book*, 49.

53 ... *hope contends with fear."* Kathleen Norris, *Amazing Grace: A Vocabulary of Faith* (New York: Riverhead Books, 1998), 30.

Chapter 4 How Much Bread Do You Have?

56 *There's a capacity.* John Steinbeck, *East of Eden* (New York: Penguin, 2002), 157; and Thomas à Kempis, *The Imitation of Christ*, trans. Leo Sherley-Price (New York: Penguin, 1952), 205.

57 ... *imagine it would go.* Matthew 15:32.

58 ... *probed further.* Matthew 15:34 Message.

58 *What did it matter.* Frederick Dale Bruner provides these observations and makes the case that the disciples' attitude toward Jesus was insolence in *Matthew*, vol. 2 of *The Churchbook* (Waco, TX: Word, 1990), 560.

61 ... *became trying to achieve it."* Toni Morrison, *Paradise* (New York: Random House, 1976), 306.

63 ... *miracle to answer.* Of course, this particular criticism is invalid if these two accounts are not dependent and rather reflect two versions of the same miraculous feeding. Donald A. Hagner, a commentator who believes Matthew (as well as Mark) preserves two versions of a single account, provides a good discussion on the possibilities for his view as well as the view for the accounts' independence. See Donald A. Hagner, *Word Biblical Commentary: Matthew 14–28*, vol. 33B (Waco, TX: Word, 1995), 449–50.

63 ... *Christian amnesia."* Bruner, *Matthew*, 560.

64 ... *were Jesus' guests at the feast.* Matthew 15:30.

65 ... *"bread of life."* John 6:35, 32.

65 ... *ing him.* John 6:35.

65 ... *come empty.* John Koessler, "Eat, Drink, and Be Hungry," *Christianity Today*, August 2007, 35.

67 ... *offered the Gentile.* Bruner, *Matthew*, 558.

69 ... *or fire, or water.* Martin Luther, "The Sacrament of the Body and Blood of Christ—Against the Fanatics," in *Martin Luther's Basic Theological Writings*, ed. Abdel Ross Wentz (Philadelphia: Fortress Press, 1959), 342.

69 ... *pinching itself."* Bruner, *Matthew*, 561.

Chapter 5 Are You Being Willfully Stupid?

72 *"And have you no fear."* C. S. Lewis, *Perelandra* (New York: Scribner, 1996), 70.

73 *. . . thick irritation.* Mark 7:18 Message.

73 *. . . or if they didn't.* The NIV translates "dull," and the NASB translates "lacking in understanding." The Greek word is *asynetos*, which literally means "without understanding, dull, foolish." The Message paraphrase ("willfully stupid") gets at the tenor of the word and the question.

73 *. . . terpret this as Jesus.* It was this sense, I think, that James Edwards resisted when he said, "Their failure to understand is not a result of stupidity" (*The Pillar New Testament Commentary: The Gospel According to Mark* [Grand Rapids: Eerdmans, 2002], 212).

73 *. . . them all the mysteries.* Mark 4:33–34.

74 *"Listen to me, everyone."* Mark 7:14.

75 *. . . Israelite who did so.* Leviticus 7:26–27.

76 *. . . the Israelites were.* Leviticus 11:1–23.

78 *. . . collapse."* Annie Dillard, *The Writing Life* (New York: HarperPerennial, 1989), 9.

78 *. . . whimsical and unexplainable.* Rainer Maria Rilke, *Letters to a Young Poet*, trans. Joan M. Burnham (San Rafael, CA: New World Library, 1992), 82.

79 *. . . mushrooming, cumbersome.* Mark 7:1–13.

80 *. . . a whiskey bottle.* Harper Lee, *To Kill a Mockingbird* (Pleasantville, NY: Reader's Digest, 1993), 47.

83 *. . . way: "Are you so foolish?"* Mark 7:18 NET Bible.

84 *. . . delight with terror.* Lewis, *Perelandra*, 69.

84 *Earth's crammed.* Elizabeth Barrett Browning, "Aurora Leigh," *Aurora Leigh and Other Poems.* Illustrated by Frederick C. Gordon (Whitefish, MT: Kessinger, 2004), 217.

Chapter 6 My God, Why Have You Abandoned Me?

86 *As being man, therefore.* Ambrose, *Exposition of the Christian Faith*, 2.7.56, available online at www.newadvent.org; and Walter Brueggemann, *Praying the Psalms* (Winona, MN: St. Mary's Press, 1993), 20.

87 *. . . abandoned me.* Mark 15:34 Message.

87 *. . . to do was die.* Mark 15:37.

88 *. . . in the lurch.* Spiros Zodhiates, ed., *Complete Word Study Dictionary: New Testament* (Chattanooga: AMG Publishers, 1993), entry 1459.

88 *. . . frightening eclipse.* Jürgen Moltmann, *The Way of Jesus Christ: Christology in Messianic Dimensions*, trans. Margaret Kohl (Philadelphia: Fortress Press, 1993), 167.

88 *. . . from me."* Matthew 26:39.

89 *. . . actually* is not *acquainted.* Hebrews 4:15 Message.

89 . . . *instant to be an atheist."* G. K. Chesterton, *Orthodoxy* (San Francisco: Ignatius Press, 1995), 145.

92 . . . *has been described.* Walter Brueggemann, *The Psalms and the Life of Faith* (Philadelphia: Fortress Press, 1995), 268.

92 . . . *the churches."* Walter Wink, *Engaging the Powers: Discernment and Resistance in a World of Domination* (Philadelphia: Fortress, 1992), 301, quoted in David E. Garland, *NIV Application Commentary: Mark* (Grand Rapids: Zondervan, 1996), 608.

93 . . . *speak this chaos.* Brueggemman, *Praying the Psalms,* 19.

94 . . . *prayers, we shall all be scandalized."* Ibid., 56.

94 . . . *understand."* Kathleen Norris, *The Cloister Walk* (New York: Riverhead Books, 1996), 11.

96 . . . *land."* Mark 15:33.

96 . . . *the older versions put it.* Acts 3:1 states explicitly that three in the afternoon is the time of prayer.

97 . . . *psalm but was also invoking.* Craig Evans, along with other commentators, considers this might well be the case. However, Evans cautions (rightly) that we not jump too quickly to the eventual vindication and triumph of the psalm without sitting in the agony of the psalm, the portion Jesus highlights. Craig A. Evans, *Word Biblical Commentary: Mark 8:27–16:20,* vol. 34B (Nashville: Nelson, 2001), 507.

98 . . . *declaring to a people.* Psalm 22:2, 19, 21, 24, 31 TNIV.

98 . . . *was most profoundly revealed."* Henri Nouwen, *The Three Movements of the Spiritual Life* (New York: Doubleday, 1975), 91.

98 . . . *will I forsake you."* Hebrews 13:5; Deuteronomy 31:6.

Chapter 7 Are You Confused?

100 *You don't believe my words.* Fyodor Dostoyevsky, *Crime and Punishment* (Ware, Hertfordshire: Wordsworth, 2000), 388; and Winn Collier, *Let God: The Transforming Wisdom of Francois Fénelon* (Brewster, MA: Paraclete, 2007), 24.

100 . . . *me." What a strange.* John 16:16.

101 . . . *it. So, yes, Jesus.* The irony is how little the confusion is cleared up even today. John did not sense the need to interpret for us precisely what Jesus meant by the "while" and "little while." Theologians still wrangle over whether Jesus was referring to a post-resurrection appearance or to his second advent, which is yet to come. I follow the interpretation that Jesus is referring to his coming death on the cross and his resurrection to follow. But it's possible I could be . . . confused.

102 . . . *words behave."* Robert Lowes, "Sunday Singing," *Jabberwock Review* (Mississippi State University) 24, no. 1 (Winter 2003), 73.

104 . . . *prodded.* Author's paraphrase of John 16:5.

105 . . . *activities a couple.* John 14:22.

105 . . . *other voices.* Brown, *Gospel According to John*, 720.

105 . . . *wrestling with his words.* This literary observation is made by Craig L. Blomberg, *The Historical Reliability of John's Gospel* (Downers Grove, IL: InterVarsity, 2001), 213.

106 . . . *all the same people you do."* Anne Lamott, *Bird by Bird: Some Instructions on Writing and Life* (New York: Anchor, 1995), 22.

107 . . . *God-Idea, not in.* Miguel de Unamuno, *Tragic Sense of Life* (Salt Lake City, UT: Project Gutenberg, 2005), available online at http://www.gutenberg.org/files/14636/14636-8.txt.

108 . . . *come."* John 16:21.

109 . . . *to live in God's world."* From N. T. Wright's lecture "The Bible and Christian Imagination," delivered at Seattle Pacific University, May 18, 2005. A transcript of the lecture may be found at: http://www.spu.edu/response/summer2k5/features/imagination.asp.

110 . . . *"they were afraid to ask.* Luke 9:45.

111 . . . *have long life before.* Fyodor Dostoyevsky, *Crime and Punishment* (New York: P. F. Collier and Son, 1917), 466.

Chapter 8 Do You Believe This?

114 *It is one of the triumphs.* Steinbeck, *East of Eden*, 448.

116 . . . *in the story.* This introduction happens in John 11. The authorship of John's Gospel is highly disputed, and firm conclusions are unnecessary because the Gospel itself makes little effort to clearly state the author's name. I tend to lean toward the traditional (though currently out of favor) view that it was John, one of the twelve disciples of Jesus (rather than a descendant of the Johannine community, for instance), who penned the majority of the Gospel.

116 . . . *ally.* Gerald Borchert suggests that Lazarus's name is probably an abbreviation for *Eleazar*, which means "God assists" (Gerald L. Borchert, *New American Commentary: John 1–11* [Nashville: Broadman and Holman, 1996], 349).

116 . . . *love is sick."* John 11:3.

118 . . . *for a corpse up until.* "The general belief was that the spirit of the deceased hovered around the body for three days in anticipation of some possible means of reentry into the body. But on the third day it was believed that the body lost its color and the spirit was locked out" (Borchert, *New American Commentary*, 354).

119 . . . *ground and now seemed limp.* It is obvious that Martha is confused and disappointed, yet she is holding on to some measure of faith in Jesus (and, in fact, some in the church have held John 11:27 TNIV: "Yes, Lord . . . I believe that you are the Messiah, the Son of God, who was to come

170

into the world," as one of the most profound Christ-confessions in the Gospels). This raw angst and conflicting emotion seem to mirror well the broken and anxious faith with which many of us struggle.

119 . . . *perceive. "This sickness will not end.* John 11:4.

119 . . . *God's Son."* John 11:4 Message.

120 . . . *them. God was working.* This larger redemptive purpose—for the redemption of others beyond Mary and Martha and Lazarus—is made clear multiple times in the narrative: for the disciples (John 11:15) and for all who would witness Lazarus's resurrection (v. 42).

120 . . . *more important to say.* John 11:25.

124 . . . *and he requested she come.* As Mary departed from her house, the Scripture tells us a crowd followed. This would have been the custom, for a crowd of mourners to stay with the bereaved. According to the Mishnah, even the poorest grieving families were required to hire two flutists and one professional wailing woman to express the family's anguish. In first-century Palestine, whenever there was a death, a crowd was sure to be there.

124 . . . *grew angry.* John 11:33.

125 . . . *description of Jesus.'* Raymond Brown offers a helpful historical and exegetical perspective on *embrimasthai* and offers something of a middle ground translation: "shuddered, moved with the deepest emotions," in *The Gospel According to John I–XII*, 425–26.

125 . . . *"groaned" (ASV).* Eugene Peterson captures what I sense to be the essence of this narrative in The Message. He does not shy from the volatile description when he paraphrases the text this way: "When Jesus saw her sobbing and the Jews with her sobbing, a deep anger welled up within him."

125 . . . *maomai, a coarse, earthy word.* In certain contexts, *embrimaomai* was used to refer to the snorting of horses, when the raging steeds would show indignation by flaring their nostrils and stomping their hooves. In each of the three other New Testament uses of a form of *embrimaomai*, it has the flavor of a harsh tone and conveys the idea of sternness.

125 . . . *"Jesus wept."* John 11:35.

Chapter 9 Why Do You Doubt?

128 *Whether your faith is that.* Buechner, *Wishful Thinking*, 23.

129 . . . *Jesus. "Don't be afraid."* Matthew 14:27.

129 . . . *to you on the water."* Matthew 14:28.

129 . . . *Jesus answered simply.* Matthew 14:29.

129 . . . *under, Peter managed.* Matthew 14:30.

129 . . . *"You of little faith.* Matthew 14:31.

130 . . . *bad habit of extracting.* Eugene H. Peterson, *Eat This Book: A Conversation in the Art of Spiritual Reading* (Grand Rapids: Eerdmans, 2006), 48.

130 . . . *portant as what is written.* Ibid.

134 . . . *because thou lovest the truth."* George MacDonald, *Lilith* (Grand Rapids: Eerdmans, 1981), 234.

135 . . . *ity."* Karl Barth, *Evangelical Theology: An Introduction* (New York: Holt, Rinehart and Winston, 1963), 122.

136 . . . *be one of 'darkness.' "* Mother Teresa, quoted in Michael Gerson, "The Torment of Teresa," *Washington Post*, September 5, 2007, A21, accessed online at http://www.washingtonpost.com/wp-dyn/content/article/2007/09/04/AR2007090401625.html.

136 . . . *instance, and the mind."* Anne Lamott, *Grace (Eventually): Thoughts on Faith* (New York: Riverhead Books, 2007), 59.

136 . . . *who pleaded, "I do believe.* Mark 9:24.

137 . . . *us from thinking."* Alfred Korzybski, *Manhood of Humanity: The Science and Art of Human Engineering* (Whitefish, MT: Kessinger Publishing, 2004), 4.

138 . . . *possibilities of God.* Frank D. Rees, *Wrestling with Doubt* (Collegeville, MN: Liturgical Press, 2001), 195.

139 . . . *that the womb was the.* Joseph Bayly, *The Last Thing We Talk About*, excerpted in "Is There Life after Death?" (Grand Rapids: RBC, 2001), 29.

139 . . . *but faith and unbelief.* Alister McGrath, *Doubting* (Downers Grove, IL: InterVarsity Press, 2006), 14.

140 . . . *it exists in and with the life.* Søren Kierkegaard, *Provocations: Spiritual Writings of Kierkegaard* (Farmington, PA: The Bruderhof Foundations, 2002), 104. This entire book, as many books of the former Plough Press, is available as an e-book, free of charge, at http://www.plough.com/ebooks/pdfs/Provocations.pdf.

Chapter 10 What Do You Want?

142 *Hope always draws the soul.* Gregory of Nyssa, *The Life of Moses* (Mahwah, NJ: Paulist Press, 1978), 114; and A. A. Milne, *The House at Pooh Corner* (New York: Puffin Books, 1992), 172.

143 . . . *who hoped for a few coins.* The Matthew account says two blind men received healing. Mark tells the story of only one.

144 . . . *of David, have mercy on me!"* Mark 10:47.

144 . . . *Jesus was the Son of David.* Mark builds ironic tension here. In 10:32–34 Jesus explained to his disciples in plain language what was to come with his death and resurrection. This was the third attempt to prepare them. However, the disciples continued not to understand what Jesus was talking about. They were *blinded* to Jesus' mission. In contrast, the blind man *sees.*

144 . . . *faith has healed you."* Mark 10:46–52.

145 . . . *erick Bruner put it, Jesus.* Bruner, *Matthew*, 746.

146 . . . *like ostriches."* George Meyer, "My Undoing," *New Yorker*, May 28, 2007, 45.

147 . . . *Christian is in fact.* St. Augustine, *Ten Homilies on the Epistle of John: To the Parthians,* Homily 4.6, at www.ccel.org, p. 630.

148 . . . *desire to unearth.* Mark 10:35–45 and Matthew 20:20–28 place the story (either by virtue of chronological reality or theological purpose) of James and John's request close to that of the healing of the blind beggar. Luke 18 references only the healing of the blind man. An interesting study might be to consider if Luke purposefully excluded the reference to James and John—and if so, why?

148 . . . *and John, approached Jesus.* The Matthew account says that it was James and John's mother who actually posed the question. Perhaps the trio were involved in the conversation with Jesus, or perhaps their mother was speaking on their behalf. It has been suggested that Matthew intended to ease the negative stigma on James and John for making such a request. Perhaps, but is it better or worse if it was their *mother* asking for them?

148 . . . *apparently were in the mood.* Mark 10:29–31.

149 . . . *in your glory.* Mark 10:37 Message.

149 . . . *be unable to "drink the cup."* Mark 10:38.

150 . . . *person Jesus healed.* Some form critics have followed Rudolf Bultmann in surmising that the added detail in Mark suggests this was not part of the original gospel narrative. However, Evans makes a good case for why this unique detail (as well as several others in the pericope) actually supports its claim to original authenticity. See Craig Evans's argument in *Word Biblical Commentary: Mark,* 129.

150 . . . *meaning "son of honor."* Bartimaeus was the "son of Timaeus," a name that literally means "son of honor." See Timothy and Barbara Friberg, *Analytical Greek Lexicon* (Grand Rapids: Baker, 2000), 380. Timaeus is a proper name, formed from a Greek word meaning "honor."

151 . . . *had angled for—honor.* Ray Stedman made this observation in his sermon from Mark 10. It is available online at http://www.raystedman.org/mark/3320.html.

151 . . . *our . . . hands/out of our pockets.* From "Grammar," copyright 1998 by Tony Hoagland. Reprinted from *Donkey Gospel* with the permission of Graywolf Press, Saint Paul, Minnesota.

153 . . . *you to where, if your soul.* Frederick Buechner, *Whistling in the Dark: A Doubter's Dictionary* (New York: Harper Collins, 1993), 117.

153 . . . *reminders of what we truly.* Hunger, in both a literal and metaphorical way, leads us, through desire, to God. "Clearly, hunger is an important guide to our well-being and enjoyment. It directs us, through desire, to that authentic creative love that belongs, in the first place, only to God" (L. Shannon Jung, *Food for Life: The Spirituality and Ethics of Eating* [Minneapolis: Augsburg, 2005], 15).

155 . . . *nature on each soul."* C. S. Lewis, *The Problem of Pain* (New York: Harper Collins, 2001), 151.

Winn Collier (ThM, Dallas Theological Seminary) is the author of *Restless Faith: Holding On to a God Just Out of Reach* and *Let God: The Transforming Wisdom of François Fénelon* and a regular columnist for *Relevant* magazine. He is leading the formation of a new church community in Charlottesville, Virginia. Collier and his wife have two sons. You may connect with him online at winncollier.com.